Special Ministries for Caring Churches

Benevolent Ministry	Child Identification Program	Conference-Call Bible Class
Depression Support Group	Employment Ministry	Homosexuals
Hospice	Hospitality	Housing for Needy Families
Mentally Handicapped	Nursing Home Residents	Physically Disabled
Pregnancy Crisis Center	Prisoners and Their Families	Public Servants
Refugees		

Robert E. Korth, Editor

STANDARD PUBLISHING
Cincinnati, Ohio 3183

Some Scripture quotations are from the HOLY BIBLE: NEW INTERNATIONAL VERSION, copyright © 1973, 1978, 1984 International Bible Society. Used by permission of Zondervan Bible Publishers.

Some Scripture quotations are from the NEW AMERICAN STANDARD BIBLE, copyright © The Lockman Foundation. Used by permission.

Library of Congress Cataloging in Publication Data

Special ministries for caring churches.

1. Church work. I. Korth, Robert E.
BV4400.S655 1986 259 86-6046
ISBN 0-87403-145-1

Contents

Introduction

More than half of the contributors to this book chose to quote a certain Bible verse. It was Matthew 25:40, "Whatever you did for one of the least of these brothers of mine, you did for me." If you recall, this is what the king told the righteous who had come before him for judgment—those who had never fed or clothed the king, or comforted him, or visited him in prison, but who had done these things for other people.

Perhaps the writers wanted to quote this verse because in some cases, their ministries brought little in the way of "tangible" returns to their congregations. No new leadership, little additional offering income, and sometimes no new members at all. They wanted to be sure we knew about the Biblical mandate for such work, as well as the personal fulfillment they have gained from doing it. But such intangible rewards may not sound like enough reason for a congregation to commit people and resources to a specialized ministry when there's so much "regular" work to be done.

To the leaders who are thinking this, I want to suggest that there are some solid, practical reasons for establishing special ministries.

First, the people with specialized needs also have a built-in agenda for ministry. If your special ministry is well-known in your area, these people may come to your church specifically for that reason. They and their families might be looking for someone who can help them and who will take the time to love and understand them. Often they are people trying to deal with a difficult problem, which means that besides being receptive to your help, they may be receptive to a saving relationship with Jesus Christ as well.

Second, ministries like these can broaden the base of contacts for your church, giving you further opportunities for evangelism. They can also serve to give your church the reputation throughout your community as a caring church. Perhaps the one thing some people know about your church is that you minister to the poor or to the physically disabled. That kind of reputation attracts people.

Third, such a ministry provides the members of your congregation with opportunities for specialized service, and perhaps training, that they will take with them the rest of their lives.

The writing of this book was done by those actively involved in the ministries. Most are not professional writers; in many cases, they are not paid staff members for the churches at which they serve. Their caring and enthusiasm for what they are doing shows through.

Getting to meet the many people involved in the work was not only the most fun and interesting aspect of putting this book together—it was also the most encouraging. If you are a caring person who sees the need for a ministry like one of these in your church, but don't think you can start one alone, meet some of these writers. Many of them have done just that.

Few of these ministries began as the result of a board decision or a church program. They began when just one or two people in the congregation had an experience with a certain problem—either themselves or someone they knew—and found ways that their church could (or couldn't) help them. Perhaps they had already received specialized training in teaching, counseling, or medicine that would enable them to conduct such a ministry. When they went to their minister or church leaders and presented their plan, they received the backing they needed. From that starting point, they have gone on to develop a ministry to help others.

In some cases the work of these individuals has expanded well beyond their expectations, with ministry organizations that are staffed and financed cooperatively by area churches, own property, and use budgets of hundreds of thousands of dollars a year. Some of these large ministries are chronicled in this book also, but all of them began with only a few people committed to the idea of helping people with specialized needs.

Opportunities and capabilities of different congregations will vary widely. They will depend on location, resources, personnel, finances, and local needs. A church in the Washington, D.C. area is well-situated to minister to tourists and to people moving in and out of that area in connection with their jobs. A church near a nursing home has the opportunity to minister to the residents of the home. A church in the middle of a region with high unemployment can respond to that need with ministries to the poor and the unemployed.

No church will find it possible to do all of the ministries presented in this book, but most of the ministries herein are within the reach of even the small congregation.

Betty Tieman, one of the contributors to this book, wrote that "Sometimes we forget that there are loving but imperfect beings within our own neighborhood who need our understanding, love, and fellowship. They seek our Lord within the church He established, and they are not always made welcome. Nothing is impossible for God; it is we who place limits as to whom His power can reach." The goal of this book is to help your church do away with some of its limitations.

Robert E. Korth
April, 1986

The names of some of the individuals in the chapters of this book, and details about their lives, have been changed in order to assure their privacy. Some of the writers could not have written about these people unless they did so.

Child Identification Program

by Judy Meneely

Judy Meneely is Children's Director at Southeast Christian Church, Louisville, Kentucky. She has been involved in various phases of the children's program there for fifteen years. She also serves on the executive board of a Christian day school. She is married and has three sons.

Benefits

Two years ago in our community, a young girl named Maria rode her bicycle to a nearby shopping mall with a friend, said good-bye, and vanished.

Her parents were recent immigrants to this country and they spoke little English. They did not have a church affiliation and had few friends. On hearing of their daughter's disappearance, they nearly collapsed. Because of their unusual circumstances, they had no support group (church, family, friends) and had trouble communicating clearly. They could not think rationally because of their emotional state. Consequently, the police and rescue teams were seriously hampered in the early hours of their search because of the lack of information and photos.

Maria might have been found—probably would have been found—but it is now two years later and the case is still unsolved.

Over two million children and youth disappear in America each year. Because of the press coverage and the emotional impact of this particular case, many schools, churches, and civic organizations in our area began campaigns to get children fingerprinted. The forms used for fingerprinting provided space to record information that authorities might find helpful in the event of a crisis.

But what do parents do with this card for safekeeping? Do they put it away at home and risk not remembering where it is if they are under a great deal of stress? Is it put in a bank safe deposit box, knowing the information will be inaccessible on weekends? Who made the fingerprints? Can they be read and classified by experts? These questions and others plagued parents in our congregation.

One day Mr. Marion Johnson, a member of our congregation, came with an idea. He envisioned fingerprinting and photographing all of our church and day school children and keeping the prints and photos on file in our church building. As he perceived it, this would provide several benefits.

1. The information would be safe because it would be kept in a locked, fireproof file cabinet in the church.

2. The information would be accessible virtually 24 hours a day.

3. One telephone call during a crisis would provide parents with the information they needed—plus they would have the immediate support of our ministerial staff and church family.

4. The information could be updated every two years.

5. The program could be valuable as community outreach, because contact would be made with families to keep information current.

6. Fingerprints would be made by fingerprint experts—professionals from the county sheriff's department—assuring parents of readable prints.

Procedures

Subsequent meetings with our senior minister and our Children's Education Committee met with a positive response. Preparation began in earnest for our Child Identification Program. We also enlisted the support of the Kindergarten and Youth Committees, since the young people they serve would be involved in the project.

Six weeks in advance

1. The Daily Preschool Director, Youth Minister, and Children's Director met to select possible dates and times for the program to be carried out. Because of the large number of children, we decided to devote Sunday-school time on two consecutive Sundays to photographing and fingerprinting, as well as school time.

2. After dates were selected, we contacted the county sheriff's department and scheduled officers to come and carry out the fingerprinting portion of the project. They agreed to supply the cards on which the fingerprinting was to be done.

3. A photographer from our congregation was engaged to take the children's pictures after they were fingerprinted. We decided on a head/torso shot so that body build would be evident, but close up enough that the picture could be cropped and enlarged to a head-only view if needed.

4. Information cards were developed (see pp. 10 and 11). These were printed on two different colors of card stock—one color for a "permanent" card, containing information that is not likely to change (birthdate, color of eyes, hair color, etc.) and another color card for information that would occasionally need to be updated (height, weight, friends, favorite foods, etc.).

5. We drew a layout of the area to be used for the project—where fingerprint tables were to be placed, where the photographer would be, and how the traffic would flow.

6. We began preliminary publicity about the Child Identification Program.

Two weeks in advance

1. We contacted four parents to act as helpers and assist during the mornings we fingerprinted. One parent wrote names of children on the fingerprint cards, one parent helped younger children clean the ink of their fingers; another parent wrote the children's names on a list for the photographer (see explanation below); the last parent was a "runner," bringing children from their classes to the project area and returning them to class.

2. We prepared a letter to parents, giving them detailed in-

White "permanent" card

Front

Date ________ CHILD IDENTIFICATION RECORD

Name (last) (first) (middle)

Blood Type: ________

Nickname

Date of Birth Sex Race

Place of Birth City State Hospital

Schools attended:(Names and addresses)

Parent (s) or Guardian(s) Name: ________

Address: ________ Zip Ph: ________

Home Church: ________

Eyes: Black ( ) Blue ( ) Brown ( ) Grey ( ) Green ( )
Hazel ( ) Maroon ( ) Violet ( ) Color Blind ( )

Hair: Blond ( ) Black ( ) Brown ( ) Red ( )

Complexion: Light ( ) Medium ( ) Dark ( ) Ruddy ( )
Freckles ( ) Dimples ( ) Other ________

Scars: (location) ________

Other marks: Pierced ears ( ) Bites nails ( ) Other ________

Back

RIGHT THUMB	RIGHT INDEX	RIGHT MIDDLE	RIGHT RING	RIGHT LITTLE
LEFT THUMB	LEFT INDEX	LEFT MIDDLE	LEFT RING	LEFT LITTLE

LEFT FOUR FINGERS	L. THUMB	R. THUMB	RIGHT FOUR FINGERS

Signature of Fingerprinter ________ Date ________

Date ________ CHILD IDENTIFICATION RECORD

Name (last) (first) (middle) Birthdate

Teeth: (Fill in number) Fillings ( ) Caps ( ) Permanently missing teeth ( ) Location________________

Broken bones (location) ________________

X-rays on file at ________________

Devices: glasses ( ) contacts ( ) dental appliance ( )

Other ________________

Eating habits: Good ( ) Fair ( ) Poor ( )

Favorite foods (3):________________

Allergies: ________________

Disabilities (limp, speech impediment, etc.)

Serious illnesses requiring spec

Illness Me

Illness Me

Hobbies:________

Places child likes to visit:________

Yellow card with information to be updated

Front

Back

Height: ___ft. ___in. Weight:________

Body build: Slender ( ) Medium ( ) Heavy ( )

Physician:________________

Address:________________ Phone________

Dentist:________________

Address: ________________ Phone________

Friends and acquaintances (list phone numbers) who might provide a lead should your child be missing:________

____

Signature Parent or Guardian

PHOTO HERE

formation about the program. The letter was distributed in all Nursery, Children, Daily Preschool, and Youth classes. Each letter had the two information cards attached to it for the parents to fill out ahead of time at home.

3. We made and posted signs in children's areas around the church building as reminders.

One week in advance

1. We bought baby wash cloths for fingerprint cleanup (these cut the greasy ink wonderfully).

2. We prepared lists for the photographer. We gave each roll of film a letter (A, B, C, etc.) and numbered each child as the negatives would be numbered. For example, the first child photographed was numbered A-1, which meant that he was on film roll A and his negative would be numbered 1. His name was written opposite the number one on the list headed "Roll A." As a cross-check his number, A-1, was also written on his card where his photo would eventually be taped into place.

3. We made signs for the project area, to lead children step by step through the processes (we used footprints with arrows on them).

The day before

1. We set up the project area at church.

2. We made sure extra cards and letters were available for visitors, absent-minded parents, or anyone who had not gotten a card.

3. We put signs in place around the project area.

Child Identification Day and the week following

1. Everything ran smoothly because planning had been done well in advance. The response was overwhelming. We had files on more than 650 children and youth by the last day of the project!

2. We used file folders cut in half in which to file our data. This doubled the amount of our filing space. Each child had his or her own file.

3. Photographs were taped hinge-style (see diagram) so that the tape did not touch the front of the picture.

4. We sent thank-you notes to parents who helped, the fingerprint team, county sheriff's office, and the photographer.

General Information

1. We plan to have the fingerprint team back once every six months in order to print those children and youth who have just recently started attending our church. Every two years our entire file will be updated with new information and photographs, but not new fingerprints.

2. There was no charge to parents. The only costs we had were for baby wash cloths, film, developing, and printing the information cards (not necessary to have this professionally done).

3. We emphasized to our parents that the files were strictly confidential—the file belongs to *them*.

4. Participation is voluntary.

5. We fingerprinted only those children with cards and parental consent.

6. We stressed filling out cards completely and carefully.

It is our prayer that no one in our church family will ever have need of any of the information we assembled. We hope it is just hours of wasted time and energy! But in the event the tragedy of a missing child strikes one of our church families, the expended time and effort may become priceless.

The Mentally Handicapped

by Betty Tieman

Betty Tieman is a member of First Christian Church in Johnson City, Tennessee, where she has been teaching her class of mentally retarded persons for nine years. Besides the class, she teaches tole painting and has exhibited her paintings. "These are the loves of my life," she writes, "next to the Lord, my husband Elbert, my three sons, a daughter-in-law, my mother, and a new granddaughter."

One of my students in class, Valerie, has webbed fingers. For many months I had a problem with this. I thought I was handling it well. I just made sure that I was on the other side of the room from Valerie when the prayer circle was formed and that I did not sit next to her in church. I just positioned myself beyond the reach of those hands.

One Sunday shortly after the death of one of our class, I arrived a little late, finding my class already in the sanctuary. I hurried in before the services started and sat down at the end of one of the pews occupied by my class members. It seemed like everything in the service reminded me of the friend I'd just lost. Though I tried to hold them back, the tears began to fall into my lap. A pair of glasses were handed to me to wipe and a small hand patted mine to help me regain my composure.

I think we were almost through the services before I noticed the webbed fingers of that gentle, kind hand. I looked up to see the beautiful smile Valerie was giving me. She'd shared my grief, had consoled me when I'd needed her. Never again have I even noticed the difference between her hands and mine.

Sometimes we forget that there are loving but imperfect human beings, maybe within our own neighborhood, who need our understanding, love, and fellowship. They seek our Lord within the church He established, but they are not always made welcome. Nothing is impossible for God; it is we who place limits as to whom His power can reach. Do we have the right to designate the privilege of being a part of His family here on earth, sharing His fellowship and His Communion, an unreachable goal in the life of the retarded?

In the past a retarded child was kept at home, hidden from view, loved but perhaps resented too, for the disruption and breakdown of the normal family structure. Society placed a stigma on both the child and the family heritage by suggesting that these differences were caused by the dissatisfaction of God for hidden sins. Swinging to the other extreme, retarded children were thought to be angels in disguise—a blessing bestowed by God on His chosen families.

In recent years, interest and concern about retardation have brought to the surface more literature, more research, and more progress in attitude than at any other time. More importantly, with the use of newspapers, TV, and education, these facts have been made available to the general public. Better informed, we are now putting the picture in proper perspective, no longer making these births an act of punishment or blessing, but simply a human event.

Beginnings and Changes

Our church class was started almost twenty years ago. It was begun by concerned elders, deacons, minister, and congregation in response to the needs of our members and the community as a whole.

In some ways, starting a class of this kind was similar to starting any new class. The planners had to appoint a committee to decide what facilities were to be used, secure sufficient teachers and helpers, provide for refreshments and supplies, make provisions for needed transportation, publicize its establishment, and seek out those who had needs for this special class. Our transportation was a taxi provided by the church, picking up those who needed a ride and taking them to church, then returning later to take them back home.

Much thought, time, and planning went into this new venture. It was a unique learning achievement, a giant step forward in recognizing that retarded people and their families have special needs that the church can help fulfill.

Workers were volunteers from the congregation, with one person serving as leader, overseeing and arranging the week's program. They used songs, handwork, a story time, memory verses and lots of motherly love to teach about God's love. This was the beginning of the class we now have in our church.

Our lessons grew as the class did, becoming more than just stories from preschool books. We started with the story of God's wonderful creation. My son, a geologist, provided many specimens of fossils and rocks and minerals. What better way to show the beauty of God's work than with these records of His creation of long ago? They could touch and share the beautiful stones with one another. They could almost feel the greatness of God and the vastness of His creation. It was exciting—like nothing we'd ever done before. How they began to grow! It was exciting to the teachers, too, to watch their interest, to hear questions that showed the amount of growth that was taking place.

Very little literature was available for our use, so we began to develop our own material for weekly lessons. We set goals and began keeping progress records. For almost a year we taught lessons geared to make our class members aware of what God had given to them when He created the world. We wanted them to be aware that everything that they enjoyed on this earth was a gift from God and for them to know God's love in the world about them.

We had easy-to-understand lessons on pleasures that God had made that they could enjoy every day—like the shade from a tree on a hot summer day or shoes on their feet in a wet, cold winter snow. As we saw their awareness of this loving God grow, the scope and depth of our lessons grew. We showed how God gave special talents to man to allow us to have comfortable houses and running water, shelter from the cold and heat, washing machines and dryers, even vacuum cleaners to clean up the messes we make. God's love was everywhere. I think we teachers even found many things we'd forgotten were gifts from God as we prepared those lessons.

Becoming Part of the Church

Just as society has changed the role of the retarded person within the social structure, so has the role of our Bible-school class changed within our church. In the beginning, class was held in an upstairs room, away from the main activities of the congregation. The room was large and comfortable and attractively arranged, but if you did not know of the existence of the class or had never delivered cookies, you might not have seen the children. Even this more isolated set-up was advanced for the time in which it was begun.

When our congregation began to plan a new building, far-sighted people designed a classroom that was large and comfortable, with its own bathroom facilities—but this time it was different. The room was located on the main floor right next to the sanctuary.

Next we began to acquaint the congregation with our class. We now had members of our class, accompanied by a teacher, take their own records to the office just as all the other classes did. We asked for Bible-school classes to allow us time during their Sunday morning sessions to share the things that were happening in our class.

We set up a workshop for interested members of the congregation. It was held on Wednesday nights for one month. In this workshop we taught what retardation was, its causes, new research being done to prevent birth defects and their handicaps, and what could be expected of our class—the good and the bad—as they began to see and be seen in more areas of the church building on Sunday mornings. We knew that we had to make the congregation understand what to expect so that they could accept the differences they would be seeing and hearing.

We used the library as a classroom for one of our lessons. Then we visited the kitchen and saw tables being set up in the gym for a church dinner. We sat in the quiet sanctuary, where the worship services were held. We arranged with the primary teachers to send two of the primary children to our classroom each Sunday morning to help take attendance and share our refreshments. Our class responded well to these visitors. The visiting children went back to their classroom to tell their friends and families about this class of special, loving people. When everyone in the primary class had visited with us, they invited us to come to a party in the primary classroom. We shared their room, their refreshments, and their lesson, but most of all their love—another giant step in becoming accepted members in God's family.

About this time our class began to attend the morning worship services. I don't think I will ever forget that first time. We did not know how the congregation would respond, nor how our class would react to the large crowds of people, singing, standing, and listening quietly. We knew that we were as ready as we'd ever be. We only hoped the congregation was ready for us. We found our seats at the front of the sanctuary (the back ones were all filled). As we waited for services to begin, all of the teachers silently asked God to let things go well and not to allow the services to be disrupted by our presence.

Our prayers were answered—our people were now Sunday morning churchgoers! How we all beamed as we left to go to our class that followed! We'd taken another step forward in God's world.

We added social graces to our lists of necessary lessons. We now had to make our students realize that to be a part of God's Sunday morning services we had to be quiet and respectful of other people.

Our congregation accepted our class and Dr. Sims, our minister, made them feel welcome. Their self-worth grew as never before—they were wanted and loved. They began to speak and smile to those around them as the service was dismissed. People began to respond with answering smiles and sometimes a handshake.

It was inevitable that as they began to get involved in church life they would begin to notice the baptisms that sometimes ended the services.

We now had to begin to teach about the sin that had entered the world and how God had given them a very precious gift—His Son, to live for them and to die for their sins. They responded well to these lessons. We began to hear in their prayers a desire to please God, to become a member of His family here on earth, and to do as He commands.

We had to listen with keener ears to what they were saying to us in class and to what they were saying to God in their prayers. We then had to relate to our minister, our congregation, and to the families of our class that some of our members were ready to accept Christ as the Son of God and their Savior.

With God's help, our first member was baptized during the morning service, March 9, 1979. I had listened to her prayers for over two years asking God to teach her what she had to know to become a member of His family. As she came into the class after her baptism, I saw her reach out to the person she thought would be the next. I heard her prayers change to "teach me how to reach my friend so that she can be baptized and be a part of your family, too."

This was a new beginning. Where once I had only had hopes for two or three, I now know that all things are possible with God. We continue to help each of our class to know and accept Christ as their Savior. Whether they can or cannot make a commitment of their life we leave in God's hands, but we know that at least they have heard about God as their loving Father. We have faith that God will take care of their eternal souls, but we also want them to have every chance to enjoy the fellowship of His family here on earth.

Teacher "Benefits"

Over the years our class has grown from six students to 32. We still have some charter members with us—now grown up and with adult needs. Many have moved away when they changed group homes or gone with their families to other congregations. Many of our teachers have moved on, too, helping to start classes in other parts of the country.

One unique aspect of our ministry is the variety of helpers and teachers who have come to us. God has richly blessed us.

Some, like myself, are volunteers from within the church.

Some are special education students, who serve with us during the school year. (Many of our college-age teachers bring their future spouses to introduce to the class). Some have come with problems they need to work out for themselves, and have found answers by helping teach our class about God's love.

Some are very young, coming before they have reached the age when they are ready to give their lives to the Lord. One such friend, Chrissy, has come to share much of her childhood with us. She began helping with our class at age five. She shared music with us when she learned to play the piano and sat with us in worship service when we were short of helpers. When she was baptized she came with her hair still wet, a beautiful smile expressing her joy, to share her experience.

We feel that each individual member of our class should decide if he or she wants to partake of Communion. Therefore we teach continuously that Jesus told us to remember the sacrifice of His blood and His body in this way. The class knows that Communion is food for our souls and not a snack to be enjoyed in the middle of church services. We use this time to remember Christ and His love. We prepare ourselves for Communion, examining what we're doing and making an effort to change our ways to please God.

One of my friends, Karen, taught me a lesson about Communion. The Communion service had just begun and Karen had reached to take a book from the rack where we were sitting. Knowing she would have trouble getting the book out I reached to retrieve it and hand it to her. She misinterpreted my action and thought I was taking it away from her. She stood up angrily and walked to the other end of the pew. I knew that if I slid over to take her the book she would probably cause a very loud commotion, so I just put the book down on the seat next to me and turned my attention to the Communion meditation. I knew that Karen had noticed the book, but I was still surprised when I felt her quietly slide next to me and lay her hand on my arm. She leaned close to whisper, "It's Communion time and I want to get right. I'm sorry."

What a beautiful way to begin a Communion service—she'd learned those lessons well, and through her actions she'd taught me, too.

After class, often the teachers linger. Joining hands we stand sharing things we'd seen about individuals, special ways that the members of the class had responded to things that had been said or done, and special prayers that had been offered in the ending prayer circle. As we stand there together we can feel God's presence. Sometimes everyone else has gone before we reluctantly disband and leave to go home. We grow in Christian love just as the class does.

Many times those from my class have shared their feelings about what it means to be a Christian. Their words help give me the assurance I need to search constantly for new ways to teach. God has been good to us. Because of the power of His love, every Sunday continues to be as new and exciting as it was when I began to teach this class.

Further Reading

H. Oliver Ohsberg, *The Church and Persons with Handicaps.* Herald Press, 1982.

Jim Pierson, *77 Dynamic Ideas for Teaching the Handicapped.* Standard Publishing, 1977.

Conference-Call Bible Class

by E. Joe Sizemore

Joe Sizemore is a freelance word processor in Phoenix, Arizona. He and his wife, Carolyn, have been married for three years. He'll tell you, "My blindness is really just an inconvenience that must be dealt with from day to day. It certainly has not kept me from experiencing life's adventures or from seeing the faithful work of God in caring for me."

Almost every Sunday Eva May attended our class and participated in the discussion. Besides being blind and diabetic, this woman, in her early sixties, also had to deal with kidney dialysis, partial paralysis resulting from a stroke, and heart problems. Her undaunted spirit was an inspiration to all of the other members of the class. Her smiling voice was a valuable contribution to the group.

Eva became a part of the class when she was invited to participate by one of the other members. Following her regular attendance for several months, I had the privilege of baptizing her into the Lord at Central Christian Church in Mesa, Arizona. Eva May has passed away since then, but not before the Lord had become a part of her life and she witnessed to His presence and saving power.

She was one of several members of a special Sunday-school class for shut-ins. The people in this group generally have some handicapping condition that makes attending services at church impractical. Even so, almost every Sunday morning finds these people ready and willing to participate in the exchange of thoughts and ideas that takes place.

This is not the typical Sunday-school class. The place in which this group meets is not a room in a building, not at all. The location of this class is a metropolis. The teacher is not standing before the group to give the lesson every week. He is at home, just as all the members of the class are. The members of this class meet together, study together, pray together, share and care together by means of that remarkable device known as the telephone.

Each Sunday morning a conference operator calls the individuals at their residences and includes each one who is able to participate in a multi-party telephone call. This whole process does not involve any special equipment being used by the individual except a telephone handset. As though it were a normal two-party call, each person is able to talk and listen to the other men and women taking part in the class.

There is, of course, a cost for this outreach ministry. The cost of a conference call is based on the number of persons participating times the number of minutes the call lasts. For us, an hour-long call among 20 people costs $16. The amount will vary depending on your local telephone exchange.

My name is E. Joe Sizemore, and it is my privilege to teach this class. It was certainly the leading of the Holy Spirit that made it possible.

In October of 1981 I began to seek a place as an assistant to a teacher of one of Bible study classes. I asked John Hendee, the Christian Education minister, how to find the place where I best fit in. He said he knew just the place for me to start, and told me about the "shut-ins" class. The teacher was one of the church's missionaries who was expecting to leave for India. After a few weeks, with me observing and participating, she turned the teaching of the class over to me and our study of the book of Luke continued.

Like the people who participate in this telephone class, I also have what is commonly known as a handicap—thought I prefer to think of it as an inconvenience. I have been blind for sixteen years. While this does not prevent me from attending regular church services, it does offer me a special advantage in relation to the teaching of the class. Because I am not able to see anyone in the first place, I have no difficulty working with this group on the phone.

I develop our lessons from Scripture, commentaries, and programmed materials that are available on recordings, in Braille, or in other special media. We have studied the Navigators' series *The Life and Ministry of Christ,* the books of Acts and Revelation, and we are now engaged in a complete study of the Bible using the Wycliffe commentary and the Holy Spirit as our guide.

A Sunday morning usually finds me waiting for the conference operator to call and tell me who will be in the class that week. After a few preliminary remarks, the lesson is presented and the members of the group are invited to ask questions, offer their own insights into the Scriptures, or just listen. We usually end with time for sharing needs and prayer requests, then we finish with a closing prayer. This is not much different from the average Sunday-school class.

Only one major problem has occurred during a lesson—becoming disconnected due to trouble at the telephone switchboard. I have sometimes gone on talking for several minutes before realizing that no one is listening. In a case like this, the people in the class know to hang up and wait for the operator to call them again. Once the call has been re-established, we resume from where it is generally agreed the lesson was interrupted.

If your church would be interested in establishing an outreach ministry such as this, it is a simple matter to get started. First you will need to determine how many "shut-ins" would be interested and able to participate in the class, and find someone capable of teaching them. If these two requirements are satisfied, then it should be possible to set up a conference call through your local telephone exchange switchboard. This can be done by calling the operator and asking for a conference operator. Following that connection, ask for the supervisor and tell that person about your church's desire to have a conference call that will be maintained from week to week at a given time. To my knowledge that is all that is needed.

I pray God's blessing on the efforts your church makes to minister to those who can best be served in this way.

I am willing to consult with anyone from your church by mail, phone, or even in person. My address is

4609 N. 50 Dr.
Phoenix, AZ 85031
(602) 846-1174

Crisis Pregnancy Center

by Sara Fudge

Sara Fudge served as the Executive Director of a Crisis Pregnancy Center in Cincinnati, Ohio. Among the duties that office included were scheduling and training counselors, record-keeping, and public relations. Sara is a member of White Oak Christian Church; she is married and has two boys.

Brenda was eighteen years old when she came to us for a pregnancy test. She had full intentions of getting an abortion if she turned up pregnant. The test turned out positive, and I gave her all the information I had about the developing baby she was carrying inside her (she was about four months pregnant). I tried to let her know we would be there to help in any way we could so she could deliver her baby. She sat quietly and listened. She didn't show much emotion. When I was done, she asked where the nearest abortion clinic was.

It has been said that the most dangerous place to be in this country is your mother's womb. At least 1.6 million abortions are performed in this country each year. Add to that the number of single mothers and the number of adoptions—the total result is a huge number of crisis pregnancies.

The stereotyped "crisis pregnancy" is a 16-year-old girl who gets pregnant out of wedlock. But any woman could have a crisis pregnancy whether she is married or not. A woman who comes to our center may be married and five children. She may be a woman in her 40's who expected to have grandchildren next, not another one of her own. She may be a girl in college or a woman going through a divorce.

Across the country hundreds of Crisis Pregnancy Centers and similar centers have been established to help women who find themselves in this situation. Our center works hard toward two main goals. One is to educate women on abortion and provide them with life-giving alternatives, support, and a constructive plan for the future. Another goal is to share the love of Jesus Christ with them.

The Lord has blessed us with life. We should not take this life for granted.

> For you created my inmost being;
> you knit me together in my
>   mother's womb.
> I praise you because I am fearfully
> and wonderfully made;
> Your works are wonderful,
> I know that full well.
> My frame was not hidden from you
> when I was made in the secret place.
> When I was woven together
>   in the depths of the earth,
> your eyes saw my unformed body.
> All the days ordained for me
> were written in your book
> before one of them came to be.
>
> —Psalm 139:13-16

What We Do

The center tries to help meet the particular needs of women experiencing a crisis pregnancy. We offer free pregnancy testing. This is generally what draws women to our center. We also advertise abortion information and referral services.

When a woman's needs go beyond what the center is set up to deal with, referrals are made. Referrals are made to adoption agencies, hospital clinics, pro-life doctors, lawyers, or other agencies that could help the women.

People in the church and community have donated maternity clothes, baby clothes, and baby items such as cribs, strollers, bottles, diapers, car seats, and other items. We then pass these on to women who need them.

Some families do not want their daughters living at home while they are pregnant. The center has a number of Christian families willing to take these girls in during the duration of their pregnancy. We call these families our "shepherding homes." It takes a very special family to open their home up to women in need. The center is privileged to have families like this.

The center and the shepherding homes work together to help the young woman build her spiritual life through a Christian environment. The program is also set up to help her to move towards a decision for her baby and a future for herself.

We also offer free childbirth classes. We have a registered nurse who volunteers her time to conduct them. There is also a nutritionist who helps during these classes.

One important thing we offer as well as the physical needs mentioned above, is our friendship.

A woman who finds herself in this situation needs someone to talk to who understands and will not judge or lecture her. She is confused and has very low self-esteem. It may be that she does not want an abortion, but because of pressures from her boyfriend, relatives, or friends, she will go ahead and have one. Later she may realize what she did to her baby and then it's too late; then she has to live with the fact of what she did. We want to educate her and give her the support materially, emotionally, and spiritually before and after she makes her decision.

About 40% of the women who walk into the center will have negative pregnancy tests. They are not pregnant. Most of these women are single and many of them are teenagers. This is a time when the volunteers have an opportunity to talk with the client about their sexuality. They talk with the women about the risks of being sexually involved outside of marriage. Pregnancy is not the only problem they are risking.

The volunteers try to share with girls what God has said about fornication. Because they have just had a "close call" with pregnancy, they are often teachable on the subject of their sexuality and are willing to change their conduct. Some girls really need someone to talk to them and encourage them to take control of their actions.

Your Church Can Help

If you have a Crisis Pregnancy Center in your area, there are many ways you can help. The most direct way that you can serve is by going through the training and volunteering to work one-on-one with hurting women. The center may also need donations of printing, advertising, office furnishings, equipment and maintenance, receptionists, secretaries, babysitters for the volunteers in the office, newsletter helpers, and shepherding homes. The center is also dependent on the financial offerings of others.

If you don't have a center in your area, you can start one. Our center was started by a woman who had compassion for the children who were being murdered in abortion clinics. She herself was adopted. The abortion issue really hit home to her—to think that she could have been one of 1.6 abortion statistics.

When she heard about the Christian Pregnancy Centers, she felt this was a ministry she could pour her heart into. She and a few friends from church got together and formed a steering committee which started the ball rolling to opening a center.

The White Oak Christian Church was a big help to the center. The steering committee turned into its board of directors. The church has also been generous in allowing the center to use the building for meetings, trainings, and childbirth classes. They have also helped with some of our printing and financial needs.

The Christian Action Council is ready to assist Christians who commit themselves to the development of a CPC. They will provide all the information you need to get started. They have assisted in starting centers all over the country. They represent the largest Protestant pro-life group in the United States. You would be working with the national staff from the CAC to start a center.

There are seven steps to follow to start a center. It would take about six months to complete. They are:

- Organize a steering committee to oversee the development of the ministry.
- Complete a questionnaire about your community resources. The CAC will send you this questionnaire. This is to find out the referral services in your area that you can use, such as doctors, adoption agencies, housing, and financial aid that are available to women.
- Incorporate the ministry as a nonprofit organization and select the board of directors.
- Solicit funds to operate the ministry.
- Appoint an executive director who implements board policy and supervises the CPC volunteers.
- Rent or purchase a facility to house the CPC.
- Educate and train volunteers who will staff the center.

The center is staffed with 30 to 35 volunteers who each donate three hours a week to the center. Each volunteer who works directly with the clients has gone through a 9- to 18-hour training program. The training covers the legal status of abortion, Biblical basis for the sanctity of human life, listening and communication skills, procedures of the center, talking to a client about abortion and her alternatives, referrals, and the role of the gospel in this ministry.

Our first training was done by a trainer from the Christian Action Council. They are based in Washington, D.C. Since the first training the center has continued with their own trainings as more people became interested in working.

The pro-life movement needs people who will speak out for the truth. Christians need to educate themselves on the issue of abortion and take a stand. Be ready to help a friend who comes to you with a problem. Spread the word that abortion is harmful to all involved.

Three months after she came to us, Brenda called the center. She had decided to keep her baby and wanted to know if we had a baby bed she could use. The center was able to help her with a baby bed, clothes, blankets, and diapers.

In November she delivered a beautiful baby girl. I received a letter from her, saying,

When I came to the Pregnancy Crisis Center to have a pregnancy test I had my mind made up, I had decided upon an abortion. But after talking to you and reading the books you gave me I slowly but surely changed my mind. . . . Now I sit and cry when I think of the joy and happiness I would be missing if I had got the abortion, and I have God and you to thank for that.

Further Reading

Curt Young, *The Least of These.* Moody Press, 1983.

For more information about starting a Crisis Pregnancy Center, contact the Christian Action Council.

Christian Action Council
701 W Broad St. Suite 405
Falls Church, VA 22046
(703) 237-2100

Ministry to Homosexuals

by Darlene Bogle

Darlene Bogle is the author of LONG ROAD TO LOVE—A True Story of Hope for the Homosexual, *published by Chosen/ Zondervan, 1985.*

She is an insurance underwriter, living in Hayward, California.

Darlene is a frequent speaker at women's groups and writer's conferences throughout the country. She has published articles in such magazines as Moody Monthly, Christian Life, Family Life Today, and The Christian Writer.

She is a member of Hayward FourSquare Church.

It was twenty minutes before my workshop was to begin. As a part of a community awareness outreach, I had been asked by the minister of a local church to teach a workshop on "How to Minister to the Homosexual." As I opened my briefcase to remove my books and handouts, I caught a glimpse of someone who had arrived early, seated in the last row.

"Hello." I moved in her direction. "My name's Darlene. I'm teaching the workshop tonight." I smiled.

"My name's Martha." Her face turned crimson, and she avoided my gaze. "I read about the workshop in the newspaper."

"Oh, you don't attend this church then?" I sat in the chair next to her. "Do you have a personal interest in this topic?"

She glanced around the room to make sure no one else

had entered. "I was involved in a lesbian lifestyle for over ten years. I've been married for almost fifteen." She spoke barely above a whisper. "No one knows . . . not even my husband."

That night, almost six years ago, the door was opened for many hours of counseling with Martha. She had been plagued with memories of her childhood and teenage years. She suffered from guilt about her homosexual involvements. Although she had become a Christian, this was a dark, secret closet that had not been opened to God's healing.

We met on a monthly basis. We began by building a Scriptural foundation for her faith in Christ and affirming her freedom from sin. She confessed and renounced all involvement physically and mentally with the homosexual lifestyle. Together we memorized Scriptures to use against the enemy when accusations would rise up against her. We prayed about the timing to share that part of her life with her husband. We counseled together on how to handle the reactions of those closest to her. They would feel hurt, shocked and deceived. We wept together at the realization of how sin had crippled her. She realized homosexuality had become a force to deal with, and that she needed to allow God's healing power to transform her inner person.

As the months passed, I became aware that she was developing a strong dependency on our relationship. Martha was looking to me for her strength and to be her conscience. I gently confronted Martha during the next counseling session.

At first she denied her dependence. She also denied any feelings of attraction. I explained that such feelings are normal in a counselor/counselee situation, and that we must be willing to discuss them. I pressed the issue, giving concrete examples of her dependency. Martha broke down and wept. She was afraid I would abandon her if I found out how strong her feelings for me had become. I assured her that in Christ, I was totally committed to her wholeness. I emphasized again that we needed to confront any unwholesome thoughts or fantasies. I suggested we bring them to the Lord and pray about them. I further suggested that we not counsel in an atmosphere that would feed an unwholesome thought life, such as secluded restaurants or even my home if it were late.

I made sure that a third party was nearby during the counseling sessions and encouraged Martha to pray that an older, mature Christian woman would come into her life who could be her friend and trusted prayer partner.

Within a matter of months God answered our prayers and Martha began to flourish in her Christian faith. She felt loved by many people. The Lord provided one older woman who was available to counsel and pray with her anytime. The new friend and her husband were also able to offer counsel when Martha shared her former life with her husband. Together they were able to work through the painful questions and keep their marriage on a solid foundation.

Martha still calls from time to time. We pray together regarding the special events in her life. God has moved her into a place of ministry in the local church body. She is now able to counsel others. With her husband's approval, Martha has shared her story of struggle and deliverance from the thoughts and memories that once held her mind captive. We've rejoiced together as she has guided others on the path of freedom. God, being an economist, has used the tragedy in both our lives to bring hope and healing to others.

I was able to teach that workshop six years ago on "Ministry to the Homosexual" because I had spent seventeen years as a member of the homosexual community. Because of my own struggle to become a whole person, and the eventual deliverance and healing that I had experienced, I was compelled to reach out and equip the church to minister to others who were still in bondage. Although my concern sprang from having been part of the lifestyle, you need not have struggled with homosexuality to have an effective ministry. It's not identifying with the sin that allows us to be a vehicle of ministry, it's identifying with Savior.

Every major city across the country, and many of the smaller communities, have areas that cater to the homosexual subculture. These areas are blatant in the acceptance of homosexuality as a viable alternative lifestyle. Less obvious, but affecting every city and every denomination, are the people who struggle with homosexual feelings. They sit in the pews Sunday after Sunday and never share their guilt-ridden feelings and never find healing for their torment. They may teach our Sunday-school classes, lead our youth or music departments, and even, in some cases, stand in our pulpits.

Preparing for Ministry

Before a local congregation can begin a ministry to the homosexual, they must have the proper attitude. The congregation must be one that proclaims clearly the Scriptural viewpoint of homosexuality—it is sin. Leviticus 18:22 commands, "Do not lie with a man as one lies with a woman." The New Testament states that "Homosexuals ... will not inherit the kingdom of God. And this is what some of you were, but you were washed" (1 Corinthians 6:9-11).

But the congregation also needs to know that no sin is beyond God's ability to redeem. The beginning steps in a sinner's healing can come through a caring Christian who does not react with shock or revulsion, but shares God's Word with him. It should not take you by surprise to find out that Satan has used a sexual sin to bring destruction in an individual's life. Our emotions are vulnerable at best, and most of us face some type of sexual temptation.

Every visitor to your service is a person with potential hurts, which may or may not include homosexuality. Each visitor should be welcomed by several in the congregation, not just the pastor. Visitors should be made aware of the services of the church, Bible studies, special ministries, and other places where they might find fellowship. As the awareness of the congregation increases to understand the loneliness of newcomers, they could invite visitors to their home for a meal or to join with other members of the church at a local restaurant after services. In the developing of a relationship, the trusting atmosphere for confession and healing is built.

This atmosphere will not come overnight, nor can it be appointed only to certain groups of people. If a church is reaching out to the community and offering unconditional love to the wounded, they won't have to advertise for a ministry to homosexuals. The word will spread. It has been said that the church is a hospital for the wounded, and as such it should be staffed with nurses and doctors. The unconditional caring and love that accepts, regardless of the background, is the type of caring that will not make a "home-missions" project out of those who enter the fellowship. Their stories will not be announced from the pulpit on Sunday mornings or prayed about on the prayer chain. People who come will find a safe atmosphere to confess their sin and find healing without making front-page news.

The leadership of the church should set the pace in establishing the attitude regarding homosexuality. They should ask God to enable the congregation to demonstrate loving compassion for people caught in homosexuality and to provide, from within the congregation, those who would work with homosexuals. Rather than an offensive outreach, their initial goal should be to provide an atmosphere where people could feel safe, accepted, and loved enough to reveal their thoughts.

The minister can help his people to determine if this is their calling by several means.

He can contact a group ministry staffed by former homosexuals. Such ministries have tapes, literature, and teams that are willing to go to the local churches and hold services.

He can locate books that would Scripturally educate the reader on the topic of homosexuality and recommend them from the pulpit or place them in the church library.

He can invite someone who has been healed from the sin of homosexuality to come and share his testimony with youth groups, women's ministries, or the entire congregation. These guests should be available to answer questions on an individual basis. The church could see firsthand that change is possible through the power of Jesus Christ.

If such an outside speaker is announced in the newspaper, you may have people from the community attending just to see what your church's approach will be.

Once the entire congregation is made aware of the nature of the problem and the hope for healing, some individuals will probably feel led to become involved in ministry to the homosexual.

Those who volunteer for such a ministry should be mature Christians with a knowledge of Scripture, strong in the faith and committed to living according to the Word of God.

They must believe in the healing power of God through the Holy Spirit; that God is able to bring wholeness to people's lives regardless of their circumstances.

They must be persons who are committed to building honest relationships, willing to make themselves vulnerable—not just to serving on a committee for ministry to the homosexual.

They must be trustworthy, and able to keep a confidence.

Steps Toward Healing

The most basic determination to make at first is whether the person desires acceptance without change. Those who are truly seeking healing will find it only in repentance and acknowledgment of the need for Christ's power to transform them. Ministries around the world are staffed by people who have found freedom from homosexuality. Although the pathway is one of hard choices, wholeness is not just an elusive dream filled with the deception of "once gay, always gay." Don't hesitate to question what their goals are or to establish guidelines for acceptable behavior.

As leaders in the ministry it will be necessary for you to make available Bible studies that will involve the person in assignments and verbal participation. They must be made a part of the church body and instructed on how to study God's Word. It will take time and commitment to put loving concern into shoe leather to walk through the months of struggle with those leaving the homosexual lifestyle.

One of the most difficult choices to be made by the person who wants to break free from homosexuality is the choice to sever all homosexual contacts and friendships. They will come up with justifications that include anything from "It's my living situation;" or "These are my only friends in all the world," or even the more spiritual excuse that "I feel led to share my new life in Christ with a former lover." These are all traps from the enemy. You must hold them to a severing of all homosexual contacts if you are going to minister effectively. Of course, you, as their new friend and spiritual support system, must be willing to make room for them in your life. They will need to relate to you as a friend, not just a counselor. I cannot emphasize strongly enough that the separation from their former lifestyle is a necessary step if they are to remain free. Encourage them to pray for their friends, but let God bring someone else to minister to them.

The counseling couple/individual should keep a close contact with the minister or leadership of the church. They can keep themselves accountable without betraying the confidences of the person they are counseling. At some point it would be wise to include the minister in on one of the sharing times. If a dependent relationship begins to develop, it should be confronted and specific steps taken to turn the dependency back to Jesus Christ. It is unhealthy for all parties concerned to have just one exclusive friendship, and the person must be encouraged to develop other friendships.

Depending upon their involvement and duration in the homosexual lifestyle, you might want to suggest professional counseling for him or her, in addition to your supportive network. It would be valuable for the minister to become aware of Christian counseling services that work with homosexuals. This should not be done as a means of rejecting the person, but as an extension of your relationship. It should always be clear that you are accepting them, but not the sinful lifestyle in which they have participated.

Condemnation is never helpful. Remember, guilt about their secret sin is what brought them to the church in the first place. Many, like my friend Martha, have lived in torment for many years because they haven't felt they could trust anyone enough to tell them. We all need the assurance from God's Word and His family that when our sin is confessed and forgiven that it is not held against us any longer.

In most cases, homosexuals were victims of sexual child abuse, incest, or rape. These are deep hurts that might be so painful they have been repressed and not even part of that person's consciousness. Also, in many cases, the homosexual has little concept of gender role behavior. A foundation must be built by peer modeling.

As they become more mature in their faith and begin to believe the message of hope for a total change, their minds will be renewed. As they internalize Scripture, they will begin to see the image of the person God created them to be. For awhile, they may feel like a tourist in a foreign country, unable to speak the language. In time and with assistance they will begin to identify with their gender role model.

One word of caution. You must not automatically believe that because their appearance has become "acceptable," that the inner wounds have been healed. One does not stop being homosexual by dropping the appearance and acts of homosexuality. A person ceases to be homosexual only when he or she is delivered from the bondage of that perversion and are cleansed by the power of Jesus Christ. Then the orientation is restored to heterosexual intention, not just placed in check. This is an ongoing process of inner healing by the Spirit of God. Your privilege is to be part of the process as you let God's healing love flow through you.

I feel one of the greatest needs in the world and in the church today is to have people who will listen and pray with you. We need others to stand with us in hope for complete wholeness.

Those called to minister to homosexuals should not be shocked if even after a commitment to Christ, the former homosexual gives in to temptation. As with any sin, they should be encouraged to confess and receive forgiveness. In the attitude of mercy and compassion, the person struggling with homosexuality should be restored to fellowship.

I strongly recommend that for at least a year, the person not be placed in any public sharing of his or her testimony.

Commitment and Limitations

As your church gains the reputation as a loving, accepting body of Christ, you will have an influx of hurting people. Those who feel led to open their homes and lives to minister to the hurting should take some precautions. If they are married, then both husband and wife should be committed to the time involvement. They should be a checks-and-balances system for one another. Make sure that the hurting person does not monopolize long hours of family time. If it is a single person who is being counseled, they could be included into family activities. Every encounter should not be a draining time for the family unit. The person should also be encouraged to join in church Bible study and prayer times.

Although I am single, I have the same number of hours in my day as everyone else. I have a full-time job. In the evenings I balance my week between ministering to others and allowing others to minister fellowship to me. I've learned the hard way that you can't always be giving of your time and energy and still maintain a strong relationship with Christ. You need to build balance into your life so that you are available for the crisis times, but that "ministry" is not your entire life. Many times, when it becomes known that you minister in a certain area of hurts, everyone with that type of problem is sent your way. As a word of exhortation to all who are starting out in ministry, any ministry, *establish your limitations.* You need to admit, even if it's just to yourself, that you cannot meet every need. Jesus Christ must be established as the source of healing, not the availability of your time schedule. Every person in the congregation can be a friend and offer fellowship without having to know the fractured life story of each individual.

In my circumstances, I have made myself available for phone counseling on a 24-hour basis. If people need to talk in the middle of the night, then I tell them to call. It would be helpful for each counselor to establish their guidelines from the beginning. If a family is involved, then the level of commitment should be worked out as a family decision.

I am convinced that if God places the desire in your heart to minister to the homosexual community, He will also draw someone from that community into your life to receive that ministering. It is He who orchestrates our lives to bring the transforming power into effect.

In every city and congregation across the land, may we hear the echo from ages past: "And such were some of you, but you were washed; but you were justified; but you were sanctified in the name of the Lord Jesus Christ, and in the Spirit of our God" (1 Corinthians 6:11).

For further information on ministries to the homosexual community, or for regional agencies, write:

EXODUS International—North America
P.O. Box 2121
San Rafael, CA 94912

EXODUS is the umbrella organization for ministries and keeps an updated referral list.

Further Reading

Don Baker, *Beyond Rejection—The Church, Homosexuality, and Hope.* Multnomah, 1985.

Darlene Bogle, *LONG ROAD TO LOVE—A True Story of Hope for the Homosexual.* Chosen Books/Zondervan, 1985.

LeAnne Payne, *The Broken Image.* Crossway Books, 1981.

Frank Worthen, *Steps Out of Homosexuality.* 1984. Available from Love in Action, P.O. Box 2655, San Rafael, CA 94911.

Employment Ministry

by Bob Dorris

Bob Dorris is a deacon at Eastside Christian Church in Fullerton, California. In March of 1982 he lost his job, the first time in 21 years that he had been unemployed. "Before I lost my job," he writes, "I really thought that those who were unemployed somehow deserved to be. God taught me how wrong I was."

In 1982, unemployment was high and going up. Jobs were hard to find. Many people my age were unemployed for the first time in their lives. The want ads were only a few pages long.

It was the church community that I turned to. This group sustained me and made me feel wanted and worthwhile. My church even offered me employment and allowed me to expend my energies constructively. I had spent much of the summer helping the staff at Eastside even as I looked for a job.

The church prayed for me. On two Sunday nights, they singled out the people who needed employment and dedicated the service to a time of prayer for us. Around that time a manufacturing company offered me a position as materials manager, which I accepted.

In the spring of 1984, several people in our congregation were unemployed. Others were underemployed, having taken positions of less challenge and pay in order to keep working at all. I went to Ben Merold, senior minister at Eastside, with concern about these people. He told me he'd support me if I'd develop a program to help them. I decided to see if I could use the resources of the church to help those who were looking for work.

The first thing we did was to put up a bulletin board titled "Employment Ministry" and posted as many job opportunities as we could find. Through the church newsletter and Sunday morning bulletin, we asked to be advised of job openings in the community. We received many listings by phone or notes. We also received large lists from companies and from Christian agencies that we know. Some people found employment through these references.

We listed the following rules for the bulletin board:

1. Job opportunities are posted for church members. While we are willing to help anyone anytime, please keep this information within the church family.

2. We are unable to check them all out. If you encounter any problems or unusual circumstances, please let us know.

3. Bring your own pencil and paper. Do not remove listings from the board. Let us know if the jobs are filled, and we will remove them from the board.

Next we tried to determine who in the church needed help and to mobilize the church membership to ministry. For a month, we inserted a form in the church bulletin to be filled out. The form read "I Need Help" on one side and "I Will Help" on the other. The response was impressive. Many more who were willing to help responded than those needing help. Even some visitors, not members of Eastside, responded.

All those needing help were contacted. Some were referred to positions that the church membership had told us about. Others were encouraged by our calls, knowing that someone cared. As we became aware of new positions, we tried to match them to those who were looking.

We found that some people really did not know how to look for a job. Many did not have resumes. Based on the offers to help, we put together a seven-week training session on writing resumes, interviewing, and conducting a job search.

The following is our schedule for our training session:

Week 1 Getting started. Review calendar and program. Guest speaker on "preparing a resume." Hand out material on resume writing. Homework: bring six ads.

Week 2 Review assignment and pair off, technical with technical, clerical with clerical, etc. Write resumes. Resumes typed by volunteer help, reproduced and made available next week.

Week 3 No meeting. Pick up resumes.

Week 4 Interview role-play and thumbnail sketch. How to answer interviewer questions.

Week 5 Meet at library. Using the library as a resource for employment.

Week 6 Prospecting—where to look, whom to talk to, how to keep records.

Week 7 Last scheduled formal meeting. Review and follow up.

After this last meeting, we will meet every other Sunday before the evening service for prayer and follow-up. Special needs anytime.

The turnout for the first session was impressive—we had two who would help for every one who needed help.

That night, Charlene Berg, a member of our congregation and a trained personnel recruiter, spoke about interviewing, preparing a resume, and personal appearance. We devoted the following nights to critiquing each other's resumes or breaking into small groups to practice interviewing each other. Those who had the skills or made hiring decisions for their companies worked with those who were looking, helping polish their interviews.

We found a couple of men who, because of their age and negative experiences in looking for jobs, were very down on themselves. One of our elders, Jerry Lauer, was able to spend time encouraging and building up these men.

Others also used their gifts and talents to help. One night we met at the local library to develop skills in using this resource. We first met with the director, Dave Snow, also a member of our church. He and his staff put together an excellent bibliography on developing a personal employment search. He even put

Survey
I WILL HELP

CAN YOU HELP? WE NEED TO DEVELOP OUR RESOURCES TO ASSIST EACH OTHER.

- ☐ PLEASE INCLUDE MY NAME ON YOUR MAILING OR CONTACT LIST. I INFLUENCE OR MAKE EMPLOYMENT DECISIONS. I WOULD LIKE TO KNOW WHO IS LOOKING AND THEIR QUALIFICATIONS.
  - ☐ I WILL HELP WITH RESUME WRITING.
  - ☐ I WILL HELP WITH INTERVIEWING TRAINING.
  - ☐ I WILL HELP IN COUNSELLING.
  - ☐ I WILL HELP...YOU TELL ME HOW.
  - ☐ OTHER

YOUR NAME____________________
ADDRESS____________________
CITY____________________
PHONE____________________

Forms used in Employment Survey

Survey
I NEED HELP

WE THE CHURCH WOULD LIKE TO KNOW WHERE WE CAN HELP. WE NEED YOU TO IDENTIFY YOUR NEEDS...SO WE CAN DEVELOP OUR PLANS.

- ☐ I AM UNEMPLOYED.
- ☐ I AM UNDER-EMPLOYED (A WORKING POSITION NOT MEETING MY NEEDS)
- ☐ I NEED HELP WITH RESUME PREPARATION.
- ☐ I NEED HELP TO PRESENT MYSELF WELL IN AN INTERVIEW SITUATION.
- ☐ I NEED HELP TO KNOW HOW TO FIND A JOB, WHERE TO LOOK, WHO TO TALK TO.
- ☐ OTHER
- ☐ CALL ME...THINGS ARE GETTING DESPERATE.

YOUR NAME____________________
ADDRESS____________________
CITY____________ZIP________
PHONE____________________

together a program about going into business for yourself if you can't find a job.

As a result of the "I Need Help/I Will Help" survey, 49 people responded who were unemployed or underemployed. We were able to help a large number of them. In addition, 61 people volunteered to help with the writing of resumes, counseling, and helping with job search strategies.

One of my goals was to use the church office as a focal point both for those who were looking and for jobs that were available. Someone in the church office would take calls and messages and match up applicants to available positions. After we concluded our formal program, I requested two copies of each person's resume. One copy would be for the church office coordinator and one for myself.

One afternoon I was at my office at work when I received a call from one of the church secretaries. A young man had come in for counseling and help. Joe had lost his job as yard foreman for a large plumbing contractor. I called him back later and asked him about his background and experience.

His job had been to lay out the various fittings and supplies for each project. This included considerable planning and effort on his part. He was also able to measure his correctness because he had to inventory the leftovers after each project.

I asked him to make up a resume, or at least write down the essentials of his education and his previous jobs. Two days later I received his handwritten resume in the mail.

That afternoon I received a call from one of our church members from his work at Hughes Aircraft. He had just become aware of an opening in his department for an Electrical Estimator/Planner. I got the name and extension of the supervisor and called him back to discuss Joe.

The supervisor seemed interested, and when I called Joe that evening, he said he thought he could handle it. I gave him the supervisor's name and number. He called and got an appointment. It must have been a good fit, because he got the job and started immediately.

As the group of unemployed people at our church grew smaller and smaller, we continued to meet one night a week for prayer and encouragement. Once in a while someone new would join us, but by the end of the summer we were meeting with only one or two.

I still receive calls from time to time for counseling or help, and sometimes just a suggestion or two.The bulletin board is still in use. But the need seems to have tailed off. Orange County is now below four percent unemployment, so for the most part, the need is gone.

The church body is a resource. It will respond to the need. As Ben often tells us about finances, "Ask God . . . tell the people." It does work!

Prison Ministry

by Allen D. Hanson

Allen Hanson is a missionary's son, Korean War combat officer, successful businessman and member of the world's largest cash grain exchange. However, in 1977 he was prosecuted in connection with grain contracts he had entered into and in 1978 sentenced to a year in prison for mail fraud and theft by swindle. He served nine months in Minnesota State Prison. The experience turned him from a passive Christian into a dynamic believer. Now in the construction tire business in Ottertail, Minnesota, he is active in prison ministries and in demand as a speaker. He shares how God changed him "from a man filled with greed, selfishness, and dishonesty, to a man anxious to help others come to a saving knowledge of Jesus Christ."

"Remember the prisoners, as though in prison with them." (Hebrews 13:3)

Going into a jail or prison for the very first time can be a terrifying experience, even if you're just going there to visit. It is difficult enough for us to witness to people we know, but the idea of going into a prison can bring instant uncertainty even to totally dedicated Christians.

Visitation

There are three ways that you can personally witness (or visit) in prison.

1. You can go yourself with much prayer, totally trusting in the Lord that His will might be done.

2. You can talk to most prisoners on the telephone with certain restrictions. You can call them occasionally or they can call you. The telephone is an excellent means by which to witness for the Lord, and you don't have to travel to the prison to do it. You can call from the comfort and safety of your own home.

3. You can also write letters to inmates. It is conservatively estimated that there are twenty prisoners waiting to write letters to someone on the outside for every volunteer pen pal willing to write back to a convict. If you want to witness for our Lord by mail, you have plenty of opportunity.

Most prisoners are not dangerous, but almost 20% of them need close custody supervision. If you obtain your leads for letter writing, telephone calls, and personal visitation from the prison chaplain or an established prison service organization, it is likely that your efforts at personal witnessing will be mutually rewarding to both you and the inmate.

There are over six thousand local lockups or county jails in America. Almost every city or large political subdivision has one. These holding facilities are used to detain men and women who are awaiting trial or legal hearings. Many of these jails are old, overcrowded, and dirty. Often short prison sentences are actually served in these institutions. All types of prisoners can be found here, from the first offender to the hardened criminal. This ministry offers an unusual opportunity right in your own hometown to reach prisoners for Jesus Christ and minister to them at a time when they are experiencing a dramatic change in their daily lives. The trauma of arrest and incarceration will occasionally jolt a new inmate into a serious evaluation of his priorities and his present lifestyle. It may be an excellent time to talk to these new prisoners about salvation.

It is easier to start a new prison ministry if two or three concerned Christians go into the jail together. Try to arrange with the authorities for a special time each week for your visit that does not conflict with regular visiting hours for the family or lawyer. Saturday afternoon or Sunday mornings are among the best available times. If you and your Christian ministry are the only visitors at the jail, you will get all the attention from both the staff and the inmates. These visits will be anticipated by prisoners who spend several weeks in the institution and they will look forward to your next call.

Less discipline trouble occurs in a prison that allows regular Christian visits. Trained law-enforcement officers know that religious visits by dedicated Christians cut the so-called "incident rate" in any jail. They will be inclined to help you even if they are not Christians themselves.

It would be beneficial for anyone considering a prison ministry to join a group going into a jail in a nearby town for several weeks to get "on-the-job" training and experience. The techniques you will acquire in a short time will make the necessary travel well worthwhile.

Here are ten tips for having an effective ministry in the local jail or area prison.

(1) Pray daily for this ministry and everyone involved in it. Start each prison visit with prayer.

(2) Keep a definite schedule without interruption. Prisoners will anticipate your regular visits.

(3) Dress conservatively. A suit coat is never out of place in jail, though a tie isn't necessary.

(4) Don't give the prisoners anything without first checking with authorities. Stay well within the established rules of the jail.

(5) Don't ask the prisoners for details about their criminal case. Often these charges are pending trial or appeal. If you learn anything about their legal status, be sure to keep it confidential.

(6) Don't expect a normal response. Conditions in jail are not normal. You are reaching the inmate with your message even if he doesn't respond immediately, so don't be discouraged.

(7) Whenever possible, arrange for a follow-up by a local church to minister to the offender after he is released.

(8) Be forgiving. The justice system is tough enough without your personal judgment and condemnation. Be a true minister of the gospel and radiate the love of God in your visit.

(9) Keep your ministry nondenominational. Most prisoners

have very little church background and do not understand theological differences.

(10) Put yourself in the prisoners' place and try to understand the way they think.

The local jail offers the average citizen a real opportunity to do mission work right in his own hometown in a ministry that most Christians neglect.

There are more than six hundred big state and federal prisons in America. Many of the same methods used in local jails apply also to big prisons, except for stricter security considerations. The prison chaplain is the key to an effective ministry in the penitentiary. Chaplains have complete control over the religious programming of a big prison. You need to work with them to be effective.

Aside from actual prison visitation, there are two other possible areas of ministry that are often overlooked: ministry to families of prisoners and to ex-offenders.

Families

Whenever someone is sent to prison, there is almost always a family left behind to wait. A prisoner's parents, spouse, brother, sister, and other close relatives represent an unusual opportunity for dedicated Christians to minister while the prisoner is in jail. There is often no better time to bring the gospel of Jesus Christ to a family than during the incarceration of one of its members. The family needs Christian love and concern. These people will be much more receptive to the gospel than usual.

There are four facts you should remember as you minister to the family of a prisoner. First, most of the necessities of daily life are furnished by welfare for needy, dependent family members of any inmate. This is part of the high cost of incarceration in our society. As Christians we can help with the special needs of the prisoner's family like moving, automobile repair, or transportation to and from prison. The daily necessities of life such as food, clothes, and housing are usually furnished by government programs.

Second, the trauma of arrest, trial and incarceration are shared by the inmate's family and friends. Relatives go through the strain of lockup and the brutal reality of the justice system with their loved ones. Although they may not show it, they will be under this strain when you contact them.

Third, relatives feel "locked up" with their loved one and will continue to have this feeling to some degree until that person is released from jail. There is no way anyone can adequately explain what it is like to have a loved one in prison without going through that experience personally. We must try to put ourselves in the family's place to understand how its members feel so we can successfully minister to them.

Fourth, a marriage is under a terrible strain when total separation of partners occurs due to imprisonment. Survival of the marriage may depend on your Christian understanding and concern. If the prisoner can come home to a loving and waiting family he has a much greater chance to avoid crime and stay out of prison in the future.

Ex-Offenders

It is conservatively estimated that more than ten million ex-offenders in the United States have served time in the nation's six hundred big prisons and penitentiaries. If you count everybody that has been arrested and jailed for a short period of time in the nation's city and county jails, that figure could exceed twenty million people. When they return, whether it be to a new community or their hometown, many local folks don't understand them and don't care much for their presence if they know anything about their prison background. Occasionally even well-meaning Christians will make sly and inappropriate remarks. The ex-offender is keenly aware of this and he is sensitive to it. He tends to withdraw from society just at a time when he really needs the love and fellowship of the local church.

The ex-offender is dealing with several personal problems. He was "busted" when many other crimes like his were overlooked. Inasmuch as only a small percentage of lawbreakers are ever caught and incarcerated, he tends to think that society has singled him out for punishment. He doesn't fully trust the justice system any more. He feels that many of the same people who were not caught for their own crimes now tend to shun him. He may have lost his wife or girlfriend while he was in prison. He doesn't have a job and he needs steady employment. Maybe he deserves everything he got from the judge for his crime, but he still feels he was "overprosecuted" because so many others went free without a prison term. Now he must deal with his righteous brother who does not understand what he has actually been through and who will not accept him.

No one can adequately explain what it is like to be locked up. A prison sentence can be a terrible thing. The trauma of arrest, prosecution and incarceration is an unforgettable experience. if the ex-offender has served a long prison sentence, he may tend to be a loner and seem indifferent at times. He may never fully return to society. However, most ex-offenders are gradually able to forget their prison experience and put it behind them. It takes at least a few months to reestablish a normal attitude and lifestyle again.

While some ex-convicts will repeat their crimes and go back to jail, nearly two-thirds of them will never enter the prison system again. This is remarkable because each one has a previous felony record and at least one strike against him already if he ever faces a judge for sentencing in the future.

A Typical Ministry

Since I was released from Minnesota State Prison in 1979, my wife and I have had the opportunity to work with numerous prisoners and their families. One such case is typical. The prisoner's name and prison location have been changed to protect his privacy.

Bill Tompkins was arrested and sent to a state prison for serious incest that resulted in pregnancy. When I visited Bill at Nebraska State Prison in Lincoln, the trauma of arrest and prosecution were evident. He was 47 years old and he had never been in trouble before in his life. He adjusted gradually to prison life and accepted our letters and religious tracts, along with a Bible we sent him. About six months after he arrived at the prison, Bill had a sincere religious experience. We could tell it in his letters and through our visits. He began to attend the prison chapel regularly.

My wife visited Bill's wife, Joan, and found that she had

completely given up all hope. She was devastated and even quit keeping house for a time. My wife helped her clean house on a couple of occasions and shared her own prison experience. At our suggestion, Joan joined an area support group near her home. Her ability to cope with the prison situation improved substantially.

Recently Bill was transferred to a halfway house near his hometown. Joan can now see him more often. Both Bill and Joan are closer to God today because of their prison experience, and our ministry definitely helped. The key is understanding and learning to cope with the prison experience. We were able to deliver an effective message of salvation and get a personal commitment. Our tools were prayer, visits, Bibles, tracts, and (in this case) a little housecleaning over a two-year period. This true story is typical of an ongoing "one on one" prison ministry.

Very few prisoners will ever return to thank you. Most of them will eventually move and put their prison experience behind them, but they will be closer to their Lord because of what you have done.

Further Reading

Charles Colson, *Born Again.* Chosen/Zondervan, 1976. Written by Colson shortly after his incarceration, so it shows the emotion of imprisonment.

Chaplain Ray, *Lady in the Shadow.* Acclaimed Books, Dallas, TX; also other books by Chaplain Ray. This book shows the trauma and problems of a prisoner's family.

Support Groups

Support groups can be formed without any special training by a dedicated host ready to hold regular home meetings for ex-offenders or prisoners' families. A one-or two-hour round table talk session is held wherever there is sufficient interest. The host will usually mail a monthly newsletter or information sheet with items of mutual interest to all attendees and vigorously solicit new members for the group.

Families of Prisoners

by Charles Lee

Charles Lee is an Associate Minister with Southeast Christian Church, Louisville, Kentucky, where he works in the area of Adult Education. He taught at the College of the Scriptures and at New York Christian Institute. He is married and has two sons.

Few people consider what happens to the family members of someone who goes to prison. When the newspapers report the disposition of a criminal case, usually nothing is said about a wife, husband, children, or other family members of the convicted person. Yet in reality the family is absorbed into the experience of incarceration, virtually "going to prison" with a loved one.

When a loved one is convicted of a crime, the family goes through a bewildering mix of emotions—shock, hurt, anger, and embarrassment just to start with. They (especially parents) begin to question themselves, even blaming themselves sometimes, wondering what failure of theirs brought about the problem. As litigation goes on, they feel a kind of gnawing, hoping against hope that their loved one will not have to endure the punishment that seems almost certain. Later, as a prisoner is serving his sentence, the slow passage of time can grind their feelings into a kind of frustration—"How did I get involved in this situation? Why me?"

We became aware of this special need through the influence

of Prison Fellowship International and the presence in our membership of those who actually have had loved ones in prison. As in most "pioneering" ministries, our efforts to establish a program for prisoners' families were guided by only a smattering of information, and were consequently destined to make a number of mistakes.

For over a year my wife and I had placed this idea before the Lord in prayer and sought the counsel of many people. We talked with fellow staff members, elders, deacons, church members, and leaders and workers involved in special ministries to inmates. We secured research work done by Prison Fellowship International and studied their guidelines on how to develop such a program. After receiving permission from the elders to initiate the program, we made lists of names of people who might want to become involved. We submitted these names to the Lord in prayer, one by one, and asked Him to give His blessing and help to this ministry.

Having secured the help of several people, we began our efforts to publicize the first meeting. We contacted local radio and TV stations and ran ads in the neighborhood papers. We also asked the chaplains in the local prisons to help us by informing the inmates of our plans. One group of inmates designed and printed up flyers to distribute to fellow inmates for mailing to their family members.

We also visited one of the prison groups and asked them how we might best serve their loved ones on the outside. Their answers fell into three major areas:

1. Give the families a means of venting their emotions and their frustrations.
2. Find ways to help them deal with the separation and to keep the relationship with the loved one alive; keep the family together.
3. Help them with their practical or financial needs.

About twelve people came to the first meeting, including two elders from a local church who wanted to observe our efforts. Others who wished to help came from Prison Fellowship and from our church. A total of five people had loved ones in prison. We refused to let this small number discourage us, because we were convinced that God values a single soul as much as He does a thousand. We conducted our meeting as planned, and today we continue to conduct meetings with enthusiasm regardless of attendance.

Sarah came to us at our first meeting telling how she had rented a house from a church shortly after her husband was incarcerated. When the church leaders found out her husband was in prison, they evicted her. She had to move so far away that she can no longer come to our meetings.

Jean's husband is innocent of the charges that have placed him in prison a second time. She comes sporadically, showing enthusiasm one day and little interest the next.

Meetings are conducted informally, usually with participants seated in a circle or around a table. Every meeting provides an opportunity for those present to talk about their personal situation in three areas: The feelings they have experienced (or are still experiencing), the practical problems they are facing (how to pay bills, repair the car, care for the children), and how the group can best work together to respond properly to each other's needs. In addition, we often invite a special guest to address the group and respond to questions. Numerous people can be helpful to such a group: probation and parole personnel, prison chaplains, judges, social workers, police, and persons involved in welfare services.

It is vital to remember that this is a ministry to those who have a special kind of hurt. As such, it is an opportunity either to encourage those who are already Christians to remain faithful, or to bring the message of God's love to those who have slipped from their earlier faith or have never become a Christian. This is not a Bible study time or a "preaching" session, but a chance to extend sympathy and love in the name of Christ. It is important, therefore, that the informality of the meetings be maintained and, unless all the participants show an earnest desire to explore some Biblical teaching, comments on Scriptural applications should be brief and discreet. There will be private times with participants later when such matters can be explored extensively.

This ministry does not have to be expensive. Costs for meetings are minimal. Needs that commonly arise with prison families include transportation to and from the prison for visitation, food, clothing and shelter, child care, and help in finding a job. If a congregation already has a benevolence program, this can be tapped for help. "Area Ministries" are developing in many urban centers and these can be approached for more extensive needs. The group members often can car pool their transportation resources to help each other.

We have really been able to help some of our people—Martha and her two daughters, for example. A third daughter received a life sentence and Martha is rearing the teenage grandson left behind. She and her daughters have come to our meetings from the beginning. Often she says, "I live for these gatherings. I don't think I could make it without coming here to find strength and help each month."

Sherry's brother recently hoped to be paroled and was sent back to serve three more years. Sherry has encouraged her aging parents to come to the group. Each time they attend, they look younger!

This is the kind of program in which the *ministry* matters more than the growth of the group. Since most inmates come from large urban areas, the success rate for growth would be higher in churches located in or around cities. The size of the congregation is of little consequence; location is more important. One or two interested volunteers could initially staff a prison families ministry effectively, and as growth occurred, thought could be given to developing staffing in some part-time professional arrangement. No special training is needed, but helpful guidelines from Prison Fellowship International are available that will save much time and energy.

It has been said that people do not care how much you know until they know how much you care. Each time someone is convicted and sentenced to prison, a family's heart has been broken, their spirit has been stifled, and their basic needs of survival have been threatened. We must ask ourselves if Jesus would care about these people if He walked among us. If we conclude that He would care, then we, His body, must care—and act.

Further Information

Basic guidelines can be secured from:

Prison Fellowship International
P.O. Box 17500
Washington, D.C. 20041-0500
(703) 478-0500

For more extensive help, write:

Mr. Ed Williamson, Texas State Director
Prison Fellowship International
P.O. Box 12964
El Paso, TX 79913
(915) 584-0375

Nursing Home Ministries

by Ruby Livengood

Ruby Livengood is a church secretary for First Christian Church, Council Bluffs, Iowa. She and her husband have been holding services at the Indian Hills Nursing Home in Council Bluffs for over twelve years.

Vada Henney was entering a nursing home to live the rest of her life.

Others were there for a wide range of reasons. Some had hardening of the arteries; their once keen minds could not grasp their "today" situations. Some were brittle diabetics on strict diets. Still others had body functions that were not what they once were. Vada was going there because her heart had grown weaker during her many years of strenuous work (she had roofed her own farmhouse at the age of 82). She needed someone to care for her and make sure she didn't overdo.

She didn't want to lose her independence, but the doctor had said she couldn't return home from the hospital if she didn't have someone there to care for her. She tried to find someone to live with her, or even just come in during the day, but no one was interested. She hadn't made many friends during her lifetime; she and her husband liked to be by themselves and didn't go places often. Since her husband's death a few years before, Vada had been very lonely. Her son and his family were living in a state far away and she didn't want to go and live with them.

That would disrupt their lives too much. She had always said she wouldn't be a burden to her son.

Her son made a quick trip back and they visited the area nursing homes. Although none were like home, they were drawn to Indian Hills. Perhaps it was because the nurse that took them around was friendlier than the others, or because this home seemed to have more alert people, or because this home didn't have the "urine" smell that the others had. Her son had packed her things, pictures, mementos, her favorite rocking chair, and the other things she would need.

Vada would be living with a roommate, since a private room was too expensive. Agnes tried to be friendly, telling her of all the activities the home provided. It was a Saturday and Agnes was just ready to go to Bible study.

Vada had never been one to go to church. When she was a child, her parents lived on a farm. It was too costly to go to church in town, 13 miles away. When she got married, she and her husband were not in the habit of going to church and nobody had ever invited them. They had been "just poor farm folks." And now here was her new roommate inviting her to go with her to Bible study and then even to church on Sunday.

Vada said, "Not this week. Maybe after I've been here for a while." She wondered aloud where they went to church, since the nursing home did not have transportation. Agnes told her that a "younger" couple, Bill and Nancy Jones, in their forties, came every week on Sunday mornings and held church services right in the nursing home's large dining room. They moved the tables back, rolled in the piano from the activity room, set up an altar for the Communion, and it was just like church.

Vada felt miserable adjusting to the nursing home that first month. Slowly Agnes got her involved in some of the activities. But when it came to church and Bible study she felt she just didn't belong. She thought that if she went, others would think she didn't know a thing and she would be embarrassed. She wished people would stop asking her to come. If it wasn't Agnes then it was her tablemates, or that preacher (he wasn't really a preacher—they called him a "layman," whatever that is, she thought) or his wife. One Sunday, the administrator of the home thought everyone might like to hear church service over the sound system. Vada enjoyed listening to the singing as she sat in her room. Then Mr. Jones talked about things in the Bible and how important it is to make Jesus our Savior. Vada didn't quite understand what he was talking about but listened intently anyway.

December came. It seemed everyone was buzzing about some activity or another. They had carolers in the hallways almost every day. The Sunday before Christmas, all of the families of the residents had been invited to come for a Christmas program put on by the church. Vada thought that it must be important, because she had overheard stories of how much fun some of the past programs had been. Vada decided she would go just to the program, if she could slip in the back so no one would notice her.

She waited until the hallways had quieted and then she slipped out of her room to the dining hall. Just inside the door there was one empty chair. She quickly slid into place.

The residents of the nursing home were putting on a pageant that told the Christmas story. There were angels in wheelchairs. Shepherds held a real cane in one hand and a staff in the other. Agnes was dressed in blue, beautiful robes as Mary, and she watched over her little great-grandchild in the manger as baby Jesus. A lot of the residents were dressed in white with red bow ties as the choir members.

That "layman," Mr. Jones, said that many children put on programs for their parents, and now it was the parents' turn to put on a program for their children. The love that flowed in that room touched Vada. She could see how the older people loved to tell the story again for their now-grown children and grandchildren. The story they had told so many times before was made special by the sacrifice of looking a little silly for the sake of love. Afterwards, fruit baskets were passed out to all the residents, not just those who attended church services.

The next Sunday, Vada decided to just "try" church. She again thought that if she sat at the back, no one would notice her. She was mistaken! There at the door was Alice in her wheelchair wearing her big, welcoming smile and shaking the hands of all who entered. Vada found a chair. Soon others involved her in conversation.

Art, wearing a leg brace, passed out the songbooks with his good hand. Bessie, with her hands shaking from Parkinson's disease, spread a cloth on the altar and put the Communion trays down gently. Marguerite wrote something in a notebook, looked up, and wrote something again. Vada decided that she was taking attendance. Emma smiled as she sat with a basket in her lap. The residents dropped coins in it as they came into the room.

Promptly at 10 a.m., Mrs. Jones said, "Good morning," and everyone started saying something that sounded like it came from the Bible: "This is the day the Lord hath made, let us rejoice and be glad in it." Then Mrs. Jones counted how many Bibles were brought to class. Vada wondered why that was so important. Next Mrs. Jones read something from the Bible and talked a little what it meant.

Then it was song time. Bernice hopped up to help others find the right page in the songbooks. Almira leaned over to Vada and remarked, "It was so thoughtful for the ministerial association to provide such nice, big print songbooks for us." Vada looked around. Everyone had smiles on their faces. She noticed that Mary, who had a stroke and was paralyzed on the left side, shared a songbook with Marie, who had a stroke and was paralyzed on the right side. Together they made a complete team. It sounded nice to hear everyone singing together.

One of the songs they sang was, "We Are One in the Bond of Love." Mrs. Jones said that was true of the church service there at the nursing home. Everyone came from different church backgrounds, but yet all were meeting together in one place because of the bond of love for Christ.

Because they were from different denominational backgrounds, they took Communion in different ways: some take Communion once a month, others once a quarter. But it was provided at this church service every Sunday. "This is the Lord's table," Mrs. Jones said. "We neither invite nor do we debar. Let all who partake do so in reverence and in relationship to their salvation in Christ."

Mr. Jones came into the room at that time. He had been

visiting in the rooms of the residents who couldn't come to church because of illness and had given them Communion. He read from the Bible, told what it meant to take Communion, and then he prayed. Ray, one of Mr. Jones' friends from his church, help pass the Communion.

Mrs. Anderson, the pianist, played what they called the "Doxology." Mrs. Anderson was not from Mr. and Mrs. Jones' church. They had looked and looked for someone from their church to come and play but no one was available. On one of her visits to the nursing home, Mrs. Anderson heard of the need for a piano player. She offered and had been playing the piano every Sunday for five years now. "How God answers prayers," they had said.

They asked Emma how much was in the offering, and then Mr. Jones said the offering goes to a children's home. A committee from the "Indian Hills" Church voted to send the money to help children learn more about Christ's love—the elderly helping the young.

Birthdays were noted, along with people that were ill in the hospital and in their rooms. Several people wrote the names down on personal prayer lists.

Then Mr. Jones gave a sermon or lesson, like the one Vada had heard over the sound system that one day. He said that Jesus loved everyone, not just those who had been church members all their lives.

Vada began attending church services every Sunday. Then she started attending the Bible study on Saturday afternoons led by Mrs. Jones. She sat there and listened but didn't say a word. If someone sat in front of her, Vada would move her chair in order to see Mrs. Jones and not miss a thing. They studied right from the Bible, verse by verse.

Every now and then Mr. Jones would bring their church bus out. All who could would pile in, and they would go for a ride to look at the changing of the seasons. Sometimes they would end up getting an ice cream cone before they went back. It was nice to get out of the home for awhile, Vada thought. Since she didn't have family close by, she didn't have the opportunity very often. Vada thought, "These people must love us, to sacrifice their time when they could be home with their families."

Once Mr. and Mrs. Jones came with the bus and took all who could go to their home for a picnic in their backyard. That was so much fun. Some nurses and orderlies from the home came along to watch over them. They roasted hot dogs and marshmallows over a well-protected open fire.

A couple of times Vada was sick and had to go back to the hospital. The only ones to visit were Mr. and Mrs. Jones and the minister from First Christian Church.

One Sunday in church, Mr. Jones announced that they would be taking names of those who wanted to go downtown to First Christian Church to a special dinner honoring all of the shut-ins. They would have a bus to take all who could ride and cars for those who couldn't climb into the bus. A pick-up would come and take all of the wheelchairs. It didn't matter if the residents weren't members of the church.

Vada overheard Mr. Jones talking to Beulah, a lady who was born with misshapen hands and feet that were of no use. Beulah was what they called "dead weight." In the nursing home they needed a lift to lift her into and out of bed. Beulah was crying because she wanted to go, but she knew that it was physically impossible for her to do so. Beulah had not been out of the home in the five years she had been there. She was like Vada; she didn't have any family nearby either. Vada felt sorry for Beulah, but also knew there was no way for them to get her there.

Then Mr. Jones did something that made Vada very upset with him. He promised Beulah that she could go. How could he do something like that? It would break Beulah's heart. The next day her fears were realized. The nurses had told Beulah she couldn't go because the church didn't have the facilities to handle her.

How mad she was at Mr. Jones! Poor Beulah. Vada almost decided to stop going to church if Mr. Jones was going to make promises he couldn't keep.

But when the special Wednesday evening came, there was Beulah all dressed up and waiting with the biggest smile of all. There were corsages for all the women and boutonnieres for the men. Mr. and Mrs. Jones came with smiles and hugs for everyone. Vada watched as Mr. Jones went over to Beulah and wheeled her right out of the car. He had arranged for a friend from the church, a strong young man skilled in lifting weights, to help Beulah in and out of the car with big doors. Vada remembered one of the things Mr. Jones had said not long ago—"With God, all things are possible."

When they got to the church they were warmly welcomed by the members and ushered to the tables (high enough for wheelchairs to slide under). Mr. Jones said that since they didn't get much choice of what to eat at the home, the people of the church would bring all kinds of good-tasting dishes from which they could choose. They certainly had done that! The banana cream pies went fast, she noticed.

After they were done eating, Mrs. Jones called all of the nursing home residents to the front so they could perform. How tickled Vada was to surprise their hosts. They had been practicing secretly for weeks with Mrs. Jones in a kitchen band. Vada was playing the washboard with thimbles on her fingers. Others had small plastic containers half-filled with corn, a rolling pin and a wooden spoon, pie tins as cymbals, an oatmeal box as a drum, and soft drink bottles half-filled with water. All were playing to the tune of "We're in the Lord's Army." The people at First Christian loved it.

When they returned to the nursing home, all of the nurses came hurrying to see Beulah and Beulah was beaming. She kept telling them, "I had so much fun. I had so much fun." It was *her* church and she had known all the time that she could go, because she said, "I prayed!" About three years before Beulah had been baptized right at the home in the bathtub! Even though she was afraid of water, she said, "I want to be in Heaven with God someday."

Vada lay in bed that night and thought about what she had missed out on for so many years. This God and His son, Jesus, that she had learned so much about, seemed to hold the answer to almost all things. He comforts you when you are sad; He hears and answers prayers; He wants His children to be happy. What a sacrifice He made—and it was for Vada, too. One thing that Vada remembered was what they had studied in Bible study for a few weeks before—it is never too late to become obedient to Christ in all things. Vada decided that night she would ask Mr. Jones next Sunday what she would have to do to become a Christian.

The story doesn't end there. Vada did confess Jesus as her Lord and Savior, God's own Son, and was baptized by Mr. Jones, "the layman," at First Christian Church. Even though Vada was an elderly lady in a nursing home, she continued to grow from a babe feeding on the milk of the Word to a faithful Christian feeding on the meat of the Word. She is gone now, but many other Vadas have come.

Mr. and Mrs. Jones are one of three couples who hold worship services at three different nursing homes in Council Bluffs. Since their congregation has more than one service on Sunday morning, they do not miss out on worship services themselves. In addition, they hold a Bible study at the nursing home on Saturday afternoons. Every few months they take the people out for an activity, like a bus trip or a cookout. Aside from the pianist, they have one or two others from church who help with the services on a regular basis. They usually have more people helping for a special activity.

Nursing home ministries can have their moments. At times you might have to step around a little puddle or pile on the floor. You have to be ever watchful for people in physical trouble (once a woman had a stroke while sitting in church). At times this ministry becomes very hard, like when one of the faithful goes to be with the Lord or one of the yet unreached does not respond.

As long as we have people like Vada, there will be a need. And we know from Jesus' parable in Matthew 20 that it is not too late.

Benevolent Ministry

by Kathy Taylor

Kathy Taylor is in her fourth year of directing the benevolent ministry at the Converse Church of Christ, Converse, Indiana. "I feel that God handpicked me for this particular mission." she writes. "You see, I've been where many of these people have walked. I've felt the despair, pain, and disappointment that many of these have felt. I've wondered at times why I've had to suffer, and now I know—because He's using me for His glory."

The following are excerpts from a letter Kathy wrote about her role in ministering to the poor in her community.

The idea came to me at five in the morning on a Sunday four weeks before Christmas, 1982. I kept thinking about Matthew 25:31-46—what could this mean to feed and clothe the needy and hungry? The following Sunday I went before our congregation with a project for our area for that Christmas season.

I outlined a drive for food and clothing, and of going through our trustees and local schools for names of families that might require extra assistance for the holidays.

The following days were busy. I contacted the school and they gave me names of families they thought would need extra help. I paid each family a visit to see what their specific needs were. Then we set aside a work day for anyone that wanted to come and help put together the Christmas boxes. We had help from within the church and a few people from the community.

Our small local newspaper covered it on the front page that day, describing what they saw as looking like "closing time Christmas Eve at a local department store." The write-up was great, though, because it totally glorified God, which you don't see much of these days!

Our first year we helped seventeen families in all. In 1983 we helped 29 families; in 1984, 34 families, and this last year 46 families in all received assistance.

The Samaritan Room

We had need for a year-round assistance program, so we found a room downstairs in our church building. Some faithful men of our congregation got together and enclosed the room. Other people hung rods, sorted clothes from a clothing drive, and organized the room. We were ready for business. Next we made some signs and put them around town explaining what we were making available to families.

We found a place called the Community Harvest Food Bank. One is in Indianapolis and one is in Fort Wayne. They're both about 70 miles from us, but worth the trip. Food there costs only 12 cents a pound, no matter what it is. Some things are even free. On our first trip we spent $108 and came home with ten times that amount worth of food. Our minister even asked me to use this for an offering meditation. God did not bless us twofold, but tenfold! Inquire around your area to see if you have such a food bank nearby.

You will need to establish guidelines on how much you give out. We give enough food for three main meals and trimmings. Staple items and non-perishables are also given. Set up a table outside your room. Talk to the people here and find out exactly what they need. Write it down and go fill their food order.

At first we had bought only basic survival items. Now since we can get things more cheaply, we splurge with a dessert mix or fancy bread mix. Some things that are necessary to stock are the things that food stamps can't buy. (This amazes me. You can buy potato chips, candy, pop, etc., but toilet paper is not a "necessity." I'd like to change a few laws!)

We allow people to get their own clothing, one-on-one in the room. We don't allow children in the room, but we do provide a place where they can go and play. Three complete outfits are given per family member. We also had a guideline to give each family clothing every three months (that hits the changing of the seasons), and food every two months, unless an emergency situation arises.

We're open on Mondays from 9:30 to 12:00.

We keep a file on each family that comes in for help. The basic questions are

Name
Address
Age
Landlord
Income
Proof of Assistance
Where They Work (or their last employment).
Place for Signature

You can check out all the information. This protects you from future problems, in case the person or family is an abuser of programs everywhere. We have encountered several of these families. We have been working with some agencies that are very helpful in this area. The first time anyone comes, we help them, taking it on faith. Then we have time to check them out before the next visit.

When you get done with your family, put their file away and get an index card. Date it and write down the items that each received at this time. Keep the index cards so you can go right to them when they come back. Much of the time you will have to use your own judgment, but be sure to establish guidelines, because these will help cut down on abuse of your ministry and help insure that you help people fairly. Sometimes people will fool you, but when they come back you can tell them that they don't qualify for more help, and why.

I believe that God says it plainly in Colossians 3:23-25: "Whatever your task, work heartily, as serving the Lord and not men, knowing that from the Lord you will receive the inheritance as your reward; you are serving the Lord Christ. For the wrongdoer will be paid back for the wrong he has done, and there is no partiality." When you get discouraged, remember your Scriptures and whom you're working for. It changes your outlook immensely.

It's nice to have someone skilled in bookkeeping help you with your project. That way you can always keep your books up-to-date and can send periodic reports to the church board. Our mission committee has us in their missions budget for aid, so they also get a report from time to time.

I don't feel it is necessary for a mission of this type to be governed by a board. Sometimes you can become so business-oriented that you lose your purpose for the ministry as it was originally intended.

Rewards

Starting a mission like this at home can be a very rewarding thing. You can actually see where your money goes, and sometimes, you can even see some beautiful results. But even if you never see results, your seed has been planted in people's lives because you've helped them in Jesus' name, and your efforts never come back void.

People enjoy hearing about your ministry, whether small or large, so periodically write an article about what's going on for your church newsletter. Many people will support your "at-home mission," because they can actually see the work for themselves and participate if they so desire.

Some of the senior high kids and coaches got particularly close to an elderly lady this past year. We had helped both her and her husband at Christmas for a couple of years. He died this past year, and since that time she lets us do things for her. We enclosed her tiny eight-foot-wide trailer and built her a little porch on the front. We got her a kerosene heater for some extra heat. I love her immensely, and I know my love is returned.

During our first Christmas we helped one family that I became very close to. The husband had cancer and several other things were wrong with him. He is about 57, and his wife is 36. They both have had hard lives, alcohol, past marriages, two children out of wedlock. They have one son about 13 years of age in a special education class.

The wife and I have a very strong relationship in the Lord.

She told me once that if she had proper clothes she'd come to church—so, what do you do but go and get them? We went to church together that Sunday; the next week she showed up with the clothes she had. I was proud of her. You see, God looks at our inner selves. It doesn't matter what we wear or what we own—it's the heart!

One Sunday after church she said she wanted to talk to me. I went to her house the following day and we went through the steps of becoming a Christian. She took her step in faith the following Sunday and became a new sister in Christ.

There's another family I'm very fond of, grandparents raising a granddaughter. They help us at the Samaritan Room each Monday. The only time we've really helped them is at Christmas for extras. She takes home some of the things we discard to make her quilts. The things you or I would normally throw away, they don't!

These are the kinds of blessings I'm speaking of. God uses you and lets you have blessings you're so undeserving of. You see, if it weren't for the faithful givers in our church, we couldn't go to these homes and do the things we do. It takes all of us working together—the faithful that hold our room up in prayer, the tithers, and the people willing to donate food, clothing, or time.

Summary

You need a room or an area not being used for anything else.

Have a clothing and food drive.

Set aside a special Sunday for an offering to get started.

Get a set of index cards in a collapsible filing box.

Make up some guidelines, based on the need in your area and your ability to help.

Make up some forms to be filled out by the families coming to you for help.

Call some of your local businesses to see if you can get discounts.

Get in touch with local and state agencies to see how they can help, with inexpensive food or clothing, references, etc.

First and most important, pray for God to send you someone to run this ministry for you! "The harvest is plentiful, but the laborers are few. Pray therefore the Lord of the harvest to send out laborers into his harvest."

God places His children carefully. I look at things through His eyes now, where once I didn't. My past hasn't been the best one, but has long been covered by the blood. It doesn't matter if you have a degree or not—just be willing and He will use you over and over.

Take Him up on the challenge and make this the most rewarding venture you've ever tried.

Ministry to the Disabled

by Jerry Borton

Jerry Borton graduated from Cincinnati Bible College in 1983. That same year, he founded Power Ministries, which exists to create an awareness in local churches of the needs and abilities of persons with physical handicaps, and to help churches develop programs to aid in their evangelism and spiritual growth.

Jerry is 26 years old, born with cerebral palsy. His chapter is about how the Edon Church of Christ helped him and his family while he grew up, and how he is now helping other churches minister to those with physical handicaps.

At least 10% of the population of the U.S. can be considered physically, emotionally, or mentally disabled. Fourteen per cent of these people claim to be Christians, which comes to several million people. But when I look around at the churches, I don't find them.

What is the reason for the lack of disabled people in churches? I have never gone to a church building and found a sign with an international wheelchair symbol and a big red "X" over it. No one has ever told me, "We don't want wheelchairs in here." But the church does react in some ways that discourage physically handicapped people. They might say something like, "Sorry, Jerry—I didn't call you about this activity because I just didn't think you'd be up to it."

A second reaction is overacceptance, or "the Brave Little

Soldier syndrome," as someone has called it. It goes like this: "Oh, Jerry, what you've done with your life is just so wonderful! I don't see how you ever could have accepted your handicap," and on and on. It can be harmful if you start believing all that about how wonderful you are; it doesn't leave you much room to be human.

A third reaction you see sometimes is a judgmental attitude: "If you only had real faith you'd rise up out of that wheelchair." These people make faith sound like coupons. If you can save up enough coupons, you can turn them in for a new pair of legs.

The fourth reaction is just a plain lack of outreach. You can see that in churches that have twenty or thirty steps going into the building. But we're talking about people who have sinned and fallen short of the glory of God, who need to become part of the body of Christ.

Although Power Ministries wasn't born until 1983, the Edon Church of Christ has been helping my family and me grow throughout my life. I was born in October, 1959 with cerebral palsy. Cerebral palsy is a condition in which the part of the brain that controls coordination and motor skills is damaged. Although I grew up in a Christian home, my disability has caused some strain on my family. Anytime a family includes a disabled individual, time and energy is diverted from normal family activities to meet the needs of the disabled person.

The church has helped me and my family in many ways. Members of the Edon Church of Christ have carried me and the wheelchair up and down countless flights of steps. They have provided rides to many youth group and church activities. Now that I am able to drive they have helped provide the financial support necessary to have a van equipped so that I can drive it.

Not only has my church made sure I attended church activities, but they were concerned about my spiritual growth. They encouraged me to be involved in a leadership position in youth group to use my public speaking ability, and to attend Bible college. The assistance of my youth sponsors and others went beyond just church-related activities by helping me with physical workouts and by also assisting me in my driver's education (complete with a side trip into a local wheatfield).

A disabled person encounters many of the same fears, frustrations and challenges an able-bodied person encounters while growing up. My youth sponsors and ministers lent an ear and occasionally a shoulder as I went through my adolescence. While I was in Bible college, my home church continued to provide encouragement and financial support as well as the opportunity to apply what I learned through two summer internships with the youth program.

While in Bible college, my goal was to become a youth minister, but I found that many churches were reluctant to hire a youth minister in a wheelchair—in many cases because they have little experience in ministering to handicapped individuals in their church. I began to see the church needed to become aware of the need to minister to the disabled population.

The people who have helped me in the church did not have degrees in special education or rehabilitation counseling. Many of them had no prior experience with handicapped people. They did have a love for the Lord and a willingness to allow Him to meet needs through them. They were not experts but they asked questions of me and my family to find out what my personal needs were and set out to meet those needs. Through the trials and triumphs, they trusted God and taught my family and me to do the same.

Three Fears About the Disabled

The first fear is that the disability might be catchy. That may seem a little silly, but it is something in the back of our minds.

The second fear is the fear of the unknown, and the person with an obvious disability represents the unknown. Most of us prefer to go into a situation where we understand exactly what's going on. It can be difficult for a person to understand the problems of a handicapped person.

The third fear is that other people's differences will help expose my own weaknesses and disabilities. We all want to believe we're pretty well put together and can handle ourselves well. When we're put in a situation in which we don't know what's going on, that bothers us.

If we can admit these fears, that's our first step in working with disabled people. If we don't admit them, we're probably not going to be good at ministering to people, disabled or otherwise.

Do's and Don'ts

Through our experience, let me offer some dos and don'ts for ministry to the handicapped.

Do get them involved. A lot of disabled people have the fear of rejection when they get into a group of people. The reason is a lot of disabled people are socially backward. For example, I was in a rehabilitation program after my freshman year at college. During that program I worked out for five hours a day; two hours in the morning and three hours in the afternoon. That program was one month long. A 13-year-old girl was also there; she was starting *her second year* of her rehabilitation program. Now that girl didn't have much opportunity to do the things normal 13-year-old girls do. So when she got out of the hospital, I'm sure she didn't act like normal teenage girls. She had some catching up to do. Those of us who are disabled have some catching up to do in some areas of our lives.

Do be creative about getting them involved. Do whatever it takes. Luke 5 tells the story of the healing of a paralytic. Jesus was at a house teaching. Some friends wanted to get the paralytic to meet Jesus, because they knew that Jesus would heal him. They went to the entrance of the house and to the windows, but they couldn't get in because of the crowd of people around. Then they went up to the roof, took the tiles off, and lowered him in.

Put yourself in the position of the paralytic. His friends were committed to him and to the Lord. Not everybody would tear the roof off a house to get you to Jesus Christ. They knew if they could get their friend to Jesus, his life would be changed forever. Now I'm not saying to take the roof off your church to get handicapped people in there, but that's the kind of commitment and creativity we need.

Don't pity individuals with handicaps. God loves them just the way they are and He wants them to use their talents for Him.

Do offer to help, but let them do what they can on their own. We need to let them know that there is a base of support for them. If they need help they can come and ask for it. But also we need to let them know that we're not stereotyping them into any categories. We're not saying that because you're deaf you can't do this or because you're blind you can't do this or because you're mentally retarded you can't do this other thing. We will let you go as far as you can go. And we'll let you try whatever you want to try and if you fail, you still have our support. We have created a culture that is afraid of failure. God wants to use our failures just as much as He wants to use our successes.

Do be patient. Many disabled people are slower than able-bodied people. It takes me about one-third longer to do things. Give a handicapped person the time he needs. Also let a handicapped person finish his own sentences. Some disabled people have a hard time talking and the urge is to grab the sentence out of their throat and finish it for them. Be patient. Do ask them to repeat if you don't understand what they said. If I say something to you and you nod your head like you understand what I'm saying and you really don't, you're really not communicating with me and you're really not ministering to me; its a form of isolation.

Do talk to them. It's funny—when I go up to the counter at McDonald's or when I go into the bank, the cashier will look out and ask the person behind me what I want.

Don't use certain words. The first word is "crippled." You hear that word and you get a negative picture. The better words are "handicapped" or "disabled."

The next words is "disease." Cerebral palsy, blindness, and deafness are not diseases. They're conditions that people have. For instance, cerebral palsy is brain damage—it gets no better, it gets no worse. You work around it. Its a condition.

The next word is "poor." I may be poor if I have only a few dollars in my wallet, but being in a wheelchair does not make me poor. Really I'm not poor anyway because I'm a child of God. Same way with "unfortunate." You see the words "victim of cerebral palsy" or "victim of multiple sclerosis," and the picture you get is that of God sitting up in Heaven and saying, "I'm going to zap that person with multiple sclerosis." That is not how it happens.

The next word is "confined," as in "confined to a wheelchair."

Think for a minute where I'd be if I didn't have my wheelchair. Proper terms to use there are "wheelchair users" or "uses a wheelchair," because my wheelchair is a tool that I use.

Don't be afraid to touch. Touch is a form of communication. I heard a woman in our church tell us that children need to be hugged at least three times a day. I think that's true for all of us. If there are persons that cannot be physically touched, because of brittle bones or surgery, they'll let you know.

Don't spoil them. I love to be spoiled. But if all you do is spoil me and give me everything, what you're doing is creating a spiritual baby. God wants us all to grow to maturity in Christ.

Do your homework. Check with federal, state, and local health agencies about services they provide. Next go to organizations for the disabled (Easter Seals, Muscular Dystrophy, and so on). Also check the public schools. In Ohio, the public school is responsible for the education of the disabled child until he's 21 years old. Check with your local university.

You also need to check with the parents. The parents are the people who can best tell you how to work with the disabled child. Many parents become experts on the disability their child has. They read every book and attend every seminar looking for ways they can help their child develop. They have some of the answers for you.

Finally, talk to the disabled themselves. We have somehow taught a whole generation not to talk about things that make people uncomfortable. We feel uncomfortable about being disabled or talking about someone's disability so we don't talk about it. We need to be willing to ask uncomfortable questions in order to be able to minister.

Further Reading

Special Ministries Counselors Handbook. Special Ministries Dept., Grace Community Church, 13248 Roscoe Blvd., Sun Valley, CA 91352.

Bonnie Wheeler, *Challenged Parenting.* Ventura, CA: Regal, 1983.

Depression Support Group

by Rose Marie Myers

Rose Marie Myers is involved in individual, marriage and family, and premarital counseling at Overlake Christian Church, Kirkland, Washington. She also is facilitator for two groups—the Depression Support Group and a Loss Support Group for those who have lost loved ones by death. After recovering from a clinical depression that lasted several years, she returned to college and earned her degree in Counseling in 1981. She is married (forty-one years) to Wayne E. Myers, a Pastoral Counselor.

Depression. In the psychological world it is considered the "common cold." As such it has reached epidemic proportion in the United States.

One out of five Americans can expect to require treatment for depression in his lifetime. In any one year between four and eight million people are depressed to the extent that they cannot effectively function on the job or that they must seek some kind of treatment. Each year in the local middle-sized church, perhaps five people will become depressed to the point of being dysfunctional for a period of time.

Depression can range from a transient, momentary feeling of emotional dejection all the way to a severe disorder that causes a person to become dysfunctional, causes a slowdown of body systems, and in some cases even leads to death.

At some point in our lives depression is going to affect each of us. This means the Christian as well as the non-Christian. No one is immune. Some will be affected only mildly, others in a severe form. Over forty-five of David's psalms reflect these deep feelings of sorrow. "The Lord is close to the broken-hearted and saves those who are crushed in spirit" (Psalm 34:18). Bible people like Moses and Elijah are classic examples of the pain incurred with depression.

Throughout history we can also find examples of all types of people who have been afflicted: Abraham Lincoln was a sufferer all his life and especially during his Civil War presidency; Winston Churchill as well. Actresses Vivien Leigh and Marilyn Monroe and Senator Thomas Eagleton suffered some variant of the illness. More recently TV personality Freddie Prinze and astronaut Edwin (Buzz) Aldrin are examples.

In the local church there will be your college professor, salesman, and the shop worker; the teenage student, the young mother, and the older mother who is no longer needed by her family. In fact, clinical depression is so prevalent in the United States that most people have a friend or relative who has suffered or is suffering some variant of the disorder.

A number of effective treatments are available for severe or clinical depressions, including several specific forms of psychotherapy, a variety of antidepressant drugs and lithium, or a combination of drugs and psychotherapy. The writer's definition for psychotherapy loosely is that which produces growth, development, and self-understanding. It can take place with a spouse, friend, pastor, psychologist or psychiatrist, as well as with a mutual self-help support group. This is where the local church can provide a ministry to its body of believers as well as to their community as an outreach.

A depression support group is designed to help a person cope with the illness of depression. It is also a means to help a person learn to live with a loved one in depression. The aim of the group is to provide help in order to survive the battle or struggle and emerge a healthier, happier, and wiser person. What better place than the local church for this to take place?

A Depression Support Group in a small local church would reduce the pastoral counseling. Cost required for this ministry is a small, bright, cheery room capable of seating approximately ten people (four to twelve is an effective group) in a circle and the training of a person to act as facilitator.

One Person We Helped

Carol, 22, was married but had been separated from her husband for several months when she started attending our support group. (Her name and other details have been altered to prevent identification.) Carol and her husband had two children, ages three and four months. Two other children, ages six and four, from her husband's previous marriage, lived with them. She and the two younger children were living with her parents when Carol became a part of the support group.

Carol's Depression Rating Scale indicated that she was struggling with depression. She stated she was very anxious over her situation. She had withdrawn from people and was compliant and passive. She couldn't seem to make decisions. Because Carol couldn't get control of her life, she was seeking help to find direction and a basis for making some decisions about her life and marriage.

Carol saw herself as a committed Christian desiring to serve the Lord, one who wished to be obedient to His word and honor Him. Fear of the future and making wrong choices was keeping her upset most of the time and not able to deal with the situations and events in her life.

By attending the group regularly, Carol began to build a trust relationship with the group and found the support she needed to begin to share her life with others who cared and were having similar problems. She was no longer alone!

The group soon noticed that Carol was trying to be all things to all people or a "people pleaser." Her frustration over not being able to meet the demands of her own high expectations was a contributing factor in her depression. She had the tendency to put herself down and be very critical of herself, making her self-concept plummet into a pit of depression. Because of this tendency, through the years she had become inhibited, keeping her feelings and emotions within her. She was not able to communicate her feelings with her husband or parents.

The group helped her to see that she had some mistaken ideas and some misplaced priorities. Though she was married, she still felt obligated to do as her parents wished, placing them on a higher priority than her husband. Her children were also on a higher priority than her husband. She was, at first, considering divorce. The group was able to help Carol's self-concept using cognitive therapy, changing the way she perceived herself to a more positive outlook. It was not long before Carol was verbalizing her feelings to the group. Then she was able to make the decision to return to her husband and seek help with marriage counseling. She would also continue to lower her high expectations of herself and others.

The Facilitator

The group leader should act as a facilitator for the group, rather than a traditional authority figure. The following are the duties of a typical group leader:

1. Responsible to enforce the contract or covenant of the group and protect the integrity of each group member.
2. Encourage each group member to identify and set individual goals.
3. Serve as a resource person, including referral to a professional psychologist if such help is needed.
4. Be available by phone or one-on-one time together for those who are experiencing an especially trying time or just need someone to listen to them.
5. Keep records.
6. Promote the group.

The facilitator does not need a degree in counseling. However, that person does need training in group dynamics and a real love and burden for hurting people. The facilitator also needs to be acquainted thoroughly on the illness of depression in order to be able to recognize what the group members are experiencing and to encourage them.

A wealth of books and training materials are available on the subject of depression and conducting a group. Some of these are listed at the end of this chapter.

Perhaps the most important part of the group leader's ministry will be to develop the art of listening. One will soon be able to recognize the symptoms and needs of an individual. The facilitator should be able to remain objective and detached while walking "through the valley of the shadow of death" with someone. The "fruit of the Spirit" (Galatians 5:22, 23) are important qualities for anyone to develop, but are even more important for a facilitator.

The facilitator should have available a type of Depression Rating Scale for each person to take privately at their first meeting, so you will be somewhat aware of where they are in their depression. A sheet with the following questions (to be answered true or false) would meet that need:

- Sad, depressed, or "empty" mood
- Loss of interest or pleasure in ordinary activities
- Sleep disturbances (insomnia, early morning waking, oversleeping)
- Eating disturbances (appetite and/or weight loss or gain)
- Decreased energy, fatigue
- Feelings of pessimism, guilt, worthlessness, helplessness, hopelessness
- Thoughts of death or suicide; suicide attempts
- Activity level slows down or increases
- Diminished ability to think and/or concentrate

An answer of five or more true would indicate the person needed help with depression.

The facilitator should also be aware of his or her limitations and establish criteria for when to refer an individual to a professional psychologist. Some reasons to make such a referral include the following:

1. If the person denies that he is depressed or that he has an emotional problem
2. If the person's depression is prolonged and shows no sign of progress (participating in the group, verbalizing new learning, better emotional state)
3. If the person causes trouble in the group by monopolizing the meetings, or if he is extremely withdrawn and refuses to participate
4. If the person exhibits extreme emotional behavior

A resource of Christian mental health professionals in both the medical profession and psychological field is an important tool for the leader to have for consultation as well as a referral source. As you build this network of support you will find they too will be sending people to your group for an ongoing support system.

Group Meetings

A covenant for the group is developed around these lines:

Purpose

Increase their knowledge of themselves; assist them to clarify changes they most want to make in their lives; and give them the tools necessary to make these desired changes.

Goals

1) Provide a trusting and permissive environment for interaction (2 Corinthians 1:3, 4).

2) Give opportunity to experiment with novel behavior (if quiet learn to speak up; if talkative learn to listen; Proverbs 23:7, 8).

3) Give opportunity to receive honest feedback concerning effects of their behavior (Philippians 3:13, 14).

4) Participants learn how they appear to themselves and others (Ephesians 4:14-16).

Dynamics

1) Support—necessary for an effective group (Ephesians 4:29).

2) Caring—"Walking in their shoes" (Ephesians 4:32).

3) Confrontation—(Hebrews 10:24, 25).

4) Self disclosure—talking openly and honestly (Colossians 3:9, 10).

5) Confidentiality—No statements and sharing that occur in the group will be shared outside the group (Hebrews 6:16; Colossians 4:5, 6).

6) Attendance—In order to keep continuity, trust, intimacy and growth, attendance and being on time is required.

The group meets weekly for approximately one and one-half hours. The first thirty minutes is spent in talking about what has been happening that week with each one present. We give encouragement when necessary and try to help with situations and events. Each person is given opportunity to express ideas, but no one is made to feel they must share at any time.

The next thirty to forty minutes is devoted to discussion on a topic that is relevant to the group. Here it is the writer's belief that the more people know about the illness, the more able they are to deal with it. Appropriate topics are guilt, anger, forgiveness, trust, and self-esteem.

We also use such video material or tapes that are pertinent to depression to assist with the discussion. The kit "Depression: Coping and Caring," by Archibald D. Hart, Ph.D., Cope Publications, 1981, provides questions and answers for discussion as well as pertinent tapes.

The remainder of the time is a devotional time or a Biblical application to what has been going on in the group that session.

Jesus commanded us to "love the Lord your God with all your heart and with all your soul and with all your mind," and to "love your neighbor as yourself" (Matthew 22:37-39). As you take the risk to become involved with souls who are hurting with this painful illness, you will be helping them to make this commandment a part of their lives, which will give them a better way of life. God will provide you with wisdom and knowledge you need and honor your efforts.

Depression is an illness of new beginnings for all who truly wish to be transformed by the renewing of their minds. God will not only reward those who are a part of the group but the facilitator also as he trusts in God to lead this ministry in the local church.

Further Reading

Group Leadership

Lawrence J. Crabb, *Basic Principles of Biblical Counseling.* Zondervan, 1975.

Leroy Eims, *Be the Leader You Were Meant to Be.* Victor Books, 1975.

Lead Out, A Guide for Leading Bible Discussion Groups. Nav-Press, 1974.

Depression

Leonard Cammer, M.D. *Up From Depression.* Pocket Books, 1983.

Nathan Kline, M.D. *From Sad to Glad.* Ballantine, 1981.

Frank Minirth, M.D., and Paul D. Meier, M.D. *Happiness Is a Choice.* Baker, 1978. This material is biblically oriented. A *Happiness Is a Choice* video series is also available.

Hospitality Ministry

by Kenneth A. Meade

Kenneth A. Meade has served as the minister of the Church of Christ at Manor Woods in Rockville, Maryland since March, 1956. He has served three times as President of the Eastern Christian Convention and coordinator of that convention from 1974 to 1985. He was Vice President of the 1981 National Missionary Convention. He served as President of the 1986 North American Christian Convention. He was granted an honorary Doctor of Divinity degree from Milligan College in May, 1986.

Every congregation needs to use the opportunities of the area in which they are located. The Church of Christ at Manor Woods is located in the suburban section of Washington, D.C. About three million people live in this metropolitan area.

Our area draws many people to us. Our congregation has been able to help many people coming here for a wide variety of reasons: for medical treatment, visiting from other countries, on field trips from schools and churches, or people moving into the area for employment. We thank God for the opportunity to minister to them all in His wonderful name.

People come from all over the world to receive medical treatment at the National Institutes of Health and other highly respected facilities. These people usually are critically ill when they arrive and often require a long period of treatment. Rarely do they have family or friends here, so the church has a wonderful opportunity (and responsibility) to minister to them in many ways.

The church usually is given short notice for the arrival of these people (when a diagnosis is made by a physician, it often requires immediate action). A typical situation is for a minister to call and inform us of someone arriving in the area that day or the next to begin treatment. Often the patient and any family members coming with them will need housing, transportation, and other physical concerns as well as spiritual and emotional support.

In April, 1980, a minister's wife in West Virginia phoned to say a young mother, Donna (age 25), would be bringing her three-year-old daughter Kelly to NIH for cancer treatment. When they arrived, we discovered they had little money to handle any of their expenses. Donna brought Kelly's twin sister and a nine-month-old son, which meant our people had to provide baby-sitting. We quickly lined up people in the congregation to handle housing, meals, transportation and visiting with them in the hospital.

It was a long period of extensive treatment. During this time, marital problems also developed within the family. Most of the burden for everything being done was resting with Donna. Our people spent much time with her, counseling and providing encouragement. To help with the financial needs of her family, we took up a love offering.

In September, 1980, the family moved to Virginia so they would be closer to NIH for treatments and the many trips they would be required to make to the hospital. When Donna and Kelly would come to the hospital, there would not be anyone available to care for the other children, so we continued to provide child care as well as financial support.

The family moved to the Maryland area in 1982. One day the physicians at NIH informed the parents they would have to make a decision whether or not Kelly's arm would be amputated. All the pros and cons were presented. They came to my office and we agonized over this decision for hours with much prayer. They decided against amputation. Thus far, this has proved to be the right decision.

In January 1983, the husband left the family. Once again we worked to handle the needs of Donna and the children. They stayed with one of the families in the congregation on many occasions. We kept close touch with them on a 24-hour basis to do whatever we could. It was difficult, but God provided through us and we were happy to serve.

In February, 1983, the husband's company transferred him to Pennsylvania and he didn't want his family to go with him. I spent many hours counseling with them whenever we could get them together. Finally, the entire family was reunited in Pennsylvania. Donna still continued to bring Kelly regularly to NIH for chemotherapy.

In 1984, the family moved to Georgia. The mother and daughter returned to NIH in early 1985. The husband had not been able to find work in Georgia, so we gave them another love offering. In February, 1985, Kelly, now eight years old, had biopsy surgery for a spot on her lung.

The family is living in Georgia at the present time and doing well both physically and spiritually. They return periodically to NIH for treatments. Our ministry will continue with them as long as necessary. They have become very special to us. We do not know what will be needed in the future, but we stand ready to help in any way we can.

Other Needs

A missionary wrote to ask us to provide hospitality for a family coming to visit the United States from the country where he was serving. A family in the congregation here opened their home to them, and others joined in to share the joy of hospitality. This family continues to keep in touch and always expresses gratitude for that act of kindness.

We also have a special opportunity to minister to many singles who come to Washington, D.C. for job opportunities. For many, it is their first time away from home and for most, it is their first time in a "big city." We work to help them find a place to live. Some come to the area to look for work, and we put them in touch with someone in the congregation who does similar work, to give them direction in how to locate the jobs and determine what opportunities are here for them. This often requires helping them with temporary housing and transportation until they are fully secured in employment.

There's also the special ministry of hospitality to groups and individuals desiring to come to the Washington, D.C. area. The Science Club from Milligan College comes every April and stays in our church building. The first year they came, our members insisted on housing them in homes. The love of our members was overwhelming and required so much of their time in eating, conversation, and the like, that they requested just to use the church building the following year. They bring sleeping bags. They leave early in the morning and return late at night. We have a commercial-type kitchen as well as eight bathrooms in the building to accommodate these groups.

We have many requests from college groups desiring to come to the D.C. area. Some are housed and fed in homes, while others desire lodging in the church building. We've hosted youth groups coming to share in national programs or just enjoy a time of sightseeing. One youth group participated in a canvass of the area with us. Another group shared outings with our youth.

There is a tremendous turnover of people in this area. Few who come here stay for a long period of time. It's very difficult to find anyone who was born here. We've had as many as forty members move out of the area in a six-week period of time. This means we are constantly working to help people who move here. For many of them, the shock of the cost of housing, as well as the complexity of the metropolitan area, makes the church a special friend and a source of help. This often requires assistance with housing, meals, and transportation when people are here on house-hunting expeditions. We spend time looking over maps with them to orient them to their church, home, and work locations.

Guidelines for Use of the Church Building

We have prepared guidelines that must be agreed to in writing by each group using the church building. Guests must provide us with specific information as requested on the form. We have found this form to be valuable as a means of clarifying what will be expected of our guests and ourselves as hosts.

1. The group leader will be provided a key to the front door of the church. Special care should be taken to determine that this door is locked each time the group leaves the building. The key is to be returned to church office.
2. Before leaving the building, please walk through to be certain all lights are turned off and thermostats have been reset to proper settings.
3. Use of the kitchen requires that it be left in a clean condition whenever the group leaves the building. All trash should be placed in proper container provided.
4. A responsible adult must be in the building at all times when the group is using the building.
5. If both boys and girls are in the group, they must sleep in separate areas of the building and be appropriately dressed when going to and from the rest rooms.
6. The church building is located in a residential area. In consideration to the church neighbors, noise should be kept at an appropriate level. A reasonable time should be set for all to be in the church building and outside noise avoided while neighbors are sleeping.
7. Any food brought in by the group should be appropriately stored. Leftovers should be either taken with the group when they leave or disposed of in a proper manner.
8. Manner of dress and language should be honorable as a Christian at all times!
9. The playing of secular rock music in the church building is discouraged.
10. Running and other roughhouse behavior is not allowed in the church building.
11. Pianos in the building should be played only by those qualified to do so.
12. No smoking or alcoholic beverages are allowed anywhere in the building.
13. Areas used are to be left in the same or better condition in which they where when use began.

14. The church office is usually open from 8:30 to 5:00, Monday through Friday. During those hours, the group leader should check in and out at the church office so the secretary will know how to handle any phone messages, etc. for the group.

15. Dates and times for use of building:

    Group will plan to arrive at the church building on (date) __________ at __________ a.m./p.m.
    Will depart from the building on (date) __________ at __________ a.m./p.m.

Name of Group____
Address: Street______________________________________
City____________________ State____________ Zip_______
Name of Group Leader:________________________________
Church or Business Phone: Area (   )_____-____________
Home Phone: (   )_____-____________
Number of boys in the group _______
(Attach a list of names and ages)
Number of girls in the group _______
(Attach a list of names and ages)
Number of adult women traveling with group _______
(Attach a list)
Number of adult men traveling with group _______
(Attach a list)

We erected the church facilities to the glory of God and we are happy to be able to share them with others. Please let us know if you have any additional questions or comments. We look forward to you being here!

Signed:________________________________ Date:__________

Note: You will be provided two copies of these guidelines. Please return one completed copy to the church office and keep a copy for your information.

Church of Christ at Manor Woods,
5300 Norbeck Road,
Rockville, MD 20853

Preparing the Congregation

The congregation must see this as a means of showing compassion in the name of the Lord Jesus. You don't see numerical results in your church attendance and it doesn't increase the financial giving. It's strictly a service of love. You must be willing to be "inconvenienced" any hour of the day.

You need at least a dozen people. When needs are long-term, requiring transportation, meals, and housing, it can be disruptive to a family's schedule and atmosphere. You need people as backup whom you can call when others are not available.

We are fortunate to have a fine lady who volunteers her full time from 8:30 a.m. to 5:30 p.m. in the church office. This greatly enhances our availability. People can call and get a response.

We have set up a group known as "Gentle Servants." Anyone in the congregation who would be available to assist families coming into our area—using whatever skills they have—is invited to be a part of this ministry. Over twenty-five people have participated in this program. They have been provided special training in "Effective Hospital Visitation" by one of the physicians in the congregation and by the minister. A psychologist in the congregation also gave training on "Skills for the Helping Relationship"—equipping people to feel more comfortable reaching out to others who may be in a crisis, in the hospital, in a nursing home, a neighbor with a problem, or in visiting or calling on behalf of the church.

A special tour was taken of NIH to acquaint people with the facility and make them feel more at ease in working with patients and their families there.

We have a budget item to help with benevolence, but it often requires special offerings of love to meet specific needs. It also costs individuals out of their personal funds. Having someone share meals with you requires purchasing extra food. When they stay in your home, it increases the utilities. If you lend them your car, they use up the gasoline. In many other ways, a personal investment is required by those providing the service.

Another part of this ministry has been for the ladies in the congregation to sew "bed pocket holders." These have large pockets in them and hang on the side of hospital bed with velcro strips. This permits the patient to keep items within easy reach. Anyone who has been in a hospital knows how difficult it is when you need items that are out of your reach. These have been very much appreciated!

This special outreach ministry has brought many rewards. First of all, the expression of gratitude from the people we've helped is a tremendous joy. It encourages a local congregation to think beyond maintenance of itself and see the broader scope of people from all over the world.

Housing for Needy Families

by Marj Norman and Joe W. Hightower

Mrs. Marguerite (Marj) Norman is Vice-President of the Human Resources Development Foundation. She is an active member of the Spring Branch Christian Church and an avid golfer . . . when she is not serving her Monday tour of duty as a volunteer at the Hospitality Apartments!

Dr. Joe W. Hightower is President of the HRDF. A professor in the Department of Chemical Engineering at Rice University, he is active in teaching, research, professional activities, and consulting. In 1982 he was awarded a Jefferson Prize in Houston for involvement in the HRDF. His hobbies include playing clarinet and making sourdough bread, which is given to all guests at the Hospitality Apartments.

The Need

Imagine that you are critically ill, perhaps not expected to live. The doctor says your only hope is to go to a faraway medical center for specialized hospital care. Costs for the treatment are staggering. In addition, you and any family members who accompany you must pay exorbitant rates for a motel room while the treatment is in progress—which could last for months.

Being from a small town, you find the city traffic terrifying and the frantic pace of life unreal. The doctors seem cold and treat you simply as a number. No one seems to care about you as a person or take the time to explain all the benefits and risks of the proposed medication. You often feel loneliness, frustration, fear, depression, and anger. What you desperately need is a group that can provide love and friendship, a person to whom you can pour out your soul, a place to go that you can call a "home away from home."

These were some of the ideas that led a group of church friends in Houston to establish the Hospitality Apartments in the late 1960's. We wanted to do something that could have an impact on the community, and there were some opportunities for service at the huge Texas Medical Center. What about transportation, food, and housing for needy families that must come to the city for treatment?

Our research determined that there was a great need for free, temporary housing for families that had been rendered "medically indigent." Uprooted from family and other normal support environments, these families are frequently forced to travel great distances to Houston for expensive and often experimental medical treatment whose outcome is at best uncertain. To reduce hospital costs, the trend in medical treatment has been in the direction of outpatient care. One wag recently said that hospital patients are being discharged "quicker and sicker." They are "dumped" on the medical center community without the resources to cope with the environment. It is imperative that relatives or friends accompany the ill person to help him or her in the therapeutic process, which may last for months. Motel/hotel charges and restaurant food can easily exceed $100 a day, this on top of all the medical costs and transportation. Often patients have not been prepared adequately for these unforeseen events, or their insurance policies have been canceled.

The problem was overwhelming. What could a small group of church friends do to make an impact on such a complex system? The enormity of the need was enough to stifle any initiative. We realized that if any impact were to be made, we simply had to begin in a small way and get on with the work. By asking some questions, we learned that a member of our congregation owned a three-lot plat located half a mile south of the medical center. He rented four dingy units in a dilapidated "army barracks" apartment building to medical and nursing students for the princely sum of $50/month, including utilities! We asked the owner if he would consider renting one of the units to our group and allow us to upgrade it and make it available to needy families. He agreed, realizing that anything we did would be an improvement to the property.

The next issue to be dealt with was how to fund this venture. Our church group involved eight families that included housewives, physicians, social workers, professors, artists, attorneys, and students. Among themselves they could manage to come up with enough money to cover the monthly rent. However, the group wanted to find a way they could receive tax credit for these contributions without forming a separate foundation. They asked the elders at the Bering Drive church if the church would pay the rent providing the group would guarantee to increase their contributions to cover the expenses. The elders were delighted to accommodate the request.

Growth

After a lot of hard work and donations of paint and furnishings from several church members, the first unit was opened on November 5, 1968. The church developed an intense interest in the project. The elders instructed us to grab the other apartments whenever they became available; somewhere they would find the money for rent. The project became a focal point around which the membership rallied. Within a few months three of the four army barracks apartments in the building were dedicated to this service. Members of the original group continued to manage the apartments, moving needy families in and out and visiting them daily to help in a variety of ways. Referrals came from hospital social workers, ministers, and previous occupants. It was soon learned that one of the most important functions of our group of volunteers could provide was a sympathetic ear. This concern has led to friendships that have extended well over ten years!

After two years the owner decided to sell the property. Realizing that the sale would most likely terminate our project in this location, we decided to incorporate as an independent benevolent foundation, seek 501(c)3 tax-exempt status, and purchase the property ourselves. A mortgage loan, a short-term loan guaranteed personally by the trustees, and cash raised mainly among church members, accounted for the $50,000 sale price. Now the fourth apartment was added to the ministry. The Bering Drive church continued to make monthly contributions to the Human Resources Development Foundation (HRDF), which allowed us to meet mortgage payments and utilities.

Maintenance was a real headache. The old building was literally falling apart. It was this circumstance that led to the involvement of the Spring Branch Christian Church. Through visiting a patient whose family was staying in one of our apartments, the minister became aware of the project. He immediately recognized the sad state of repairs and suggested that one of their classes dedicate a "work day" to upgrade the building. On a beautiful October day in 1974 about 25 skilled workers combined their talents to repaint and refurbish the entire building. Other classes at the church redecorated the insides of the units. This activity established a precedent; since then the "work day" has become an annual event. Occasionally a problem arose that could not be handled by someone in the church, but only rarely did we need paid professionals to do maintenance work. As a direct result of personal involvement of members in this project, the Spring Branch church began making monthly contributions to the HRDF. Three of its members are now Foundation trustees. Other classes provide funds for specific items, as did the Ladies' Bible Class at the Bering Drive church.

In 1977 a third church, Covenant Baptist Church, also began supporting this project. Nine other church groups have since made donations to the HRDF, and it was not long before the 20-year, $30,000 property mortgage was retired—12 years early!

The Foundation labeled the purchase of the property *Phase One* and began to investigate the possibilities of expanding the project. An architect donated his services to prepare plans for a new building on a vacant part of the same property. Realizing that such plans were beyond the capabilities of the churches involved, the HRDF trustees began trying to raise money from private foundations, corporations, and individuals in the Houston area. After about $120,000 of the required $180,000 had been secured, the contract was signed and work began on *Phase Two.* By the time the seven new units and laundry room were opened on April 14, 1982, all the building funds had been raised. Spurred by this success, plans for *Phase Three* (eight more units built in place of the army barracks) were immediately activated, and the $225,000 building opened on July 16, 1983, again all paid for. Since this date we have operated with 15 new apartments and have served almost 1,000 families from 44 U.S. states and 32 foreign countries.

The HRDF is now involved in its most ambitious project, that being to expand the Hospitality Apartments to 21 units. All but $20,000 of the $300,000 project has been raised, and construction of *Phase Four* should be completed by mid-1986. The largest single contribution, $50,000, came from the Houston Project Committee of the St. Luke's United Methodist Church in Houston.

Personnel

The management of the Hospitality Apartments is done strictly by volunteers. Never in our history has a single person received pay for any service. We have no paid fund raisers, nor has the Foundation ever hired a secretary. Every penny received by the HRDF goes directly into the services provided.

A group of 18 trustees are elected annually to formulate policy for the Foundation. These are not people who are well known in Houston; they are people who have special skills that are required to manage the project. For example, the Foundation secretary is an attorney for a large law firm in Houston; the treasurer is a CPA with his own accounting firm. One trustee is a commercial artist who takes on the responsibility of planning graphical material. Others are medical doctors with useful connections in the Texas Medical Center. Our Volunteer Coordinator dedicates a large fraction of her time to making sure the HRDF is well run from day to day. A key element is the monthly newsletter called *The Volunteer,* which is edited by another trustee.The president has his own word processor, which makes it easy for him to handle the substantial amount of correspondence. Being a professor in the nearby Rice University, his schedule is sufficiently flexible that he can make frequent trips to the Hospitality Apartments to encourage volunteers, visit the guests, and deal with any problems that occasionally arise. Each of these people contributes in a unique and vital way to making this project successful.

A second layer of official involvement is through the twenty advisors. Some of these people are well-known in the Houston community, and others are representatives of churches and various groups that provide support. Considering the type of services, it is not surprising that one advisor is the president of the Texas Medical Center, Inc. Rarely do these people become directly involved in the day-to-day operations, but their backing helps give the project credibility in the city. Our advisor who represents the American Red Cross has been instrumental in referring several people who have become useful volunteers . . . some even trustees.

Most important are the community volunteers, several of whom are also trustees or advisors. At present about 60 of these dedicated people commit large fractions of their time to staffing the Volunteer Office and ministering directly to the needs of our medically indigent guests. Each weekday there are two shifts of people (9 to 12 and 12 to 3) who usually work in pairs. They answer the telephone, put people on the waiting list, move guests in and out, distribute food each Wednesday, answer questions, take people grocery shopping, and more—the list could go on indefinitely. Each person has some unique gift that he or she can bring to bear on the special needs of our guests, about 12% of whom do not survive the treatment. For example, the president gives a loaf of his homemade sourdough bread to each family when they enter an apartment. Others may offer to care for children when a parent is undergoing treatment or occasionally invite families to their homes for dinner. These volunteers are providing a bridge across the enormous gap that exists between the hospital patients and the Houston community. Their efforts make it possible for guests to survive in the cold, unknown, and often frightening environment of a distant medical center.

A special note should be added about the resident manager.

For the first 12 years the trustees did most of the work in running the apartments. When the seven new *Phase Two* units were opened in 1982, the system of community volunteers was instituted. Upon increasing the number of apartments to 15 the next year, we realized that someone needed to be there all the time to handle problems that may arise at night. Security is an significant concern in the area where the apartments are located.

One of the guests is a recently retired policeman from Amarillo who is involved in a long-term experimental outpatient treatment for cancer. Since he and his lovely wife interacted beautifully with the other guests, we asked them to serve as resident managers. They jumped at the opportunity and have done a fantastic job. Although we provide a place to live and a telephone, we do not pay the resident manager. Ken, who will probably be on periodic chemotherapy for the rest of his life, is doing extremely well. Our guess is that part of his progress is due to the sense of purpose he derives from helping others through this ministry. In fact, one day Ken said that he thought God had put them on the earth specifically to do this job. We've told Ken that if he ever gets fully cured, he is not to tell us!

Some Criteria for Success

First there must be a well-documented need. Second, some person or small group must be willing to take the initiative to get things rolling. The person must have leadership qualities and an ability to persuade others to become involved. He must also be willing to put in an enormous amount of time. In our case, the president has averaged spending about 20 hours per week on this project.

The critical step is to get started. One should not try to solve all the problems in advance. Begin the project and deal with the problems individually as they arise. Start in a small way and then expand as the need arises and resources permit. It is impossible to see the exact direction any project of this type will take in future years. Seventeen years ago we had no idea that by 1986 we would be able to minister to 200 families per year. Indeed the Lord has blessed our needy guests (and us as well!) more than we could have ever dreamed at the outset.

Another important criterion for success is to pay as you go. Except for the initial mortgage loan when the property was purchased, we have been able to raise the money in advance for each of the expansions. If the project is worthwhile, it is easy to interest others in providing funds. Potential donors recognize and appreciate the time that you and others invest in making this project work.

Although our project "sells itself," it still takes a lot of effort to make sure the right people are informed about its existence. Public recognition is very important because it lends credibility to the work. For example, considerable money came in as result of our president being awarded a Jefferson Prize for Public Service in Houston. Media announcements (newspaper articles, television spots, etc.) are useful not only to help in raising funds, but to interest people in serving as volunteers.

It is also important to have the support of churches that have carefully investigated and put their stamp of approval on your project. Frequently potential donors will put their personal support behind projects they know have been sanctioned by churches. So many people seek funds for worthless causes that a considerable amount of time can be consumed in checking out the various groups. By supporting a specific project, a church can eliminate a lot of the "legwork" that would be otherwise required by an individual donor.

Do not accept government funding! If at all possible, keep your benevolent project free of federal, state, or municipal funding. With such funding come all kinds of strings and reporting requirements that will greatly increase your operating costs. By remaining independent, you will be free to make quick policy changes that will increase the effectiveness of your operations. With government funding come government controls!

Our project has required about a million dollars for capital and operating funds during the last 17 years. Based on the $30 per day these needy guests might have paid for a hotel room, already our Hospitality Apartments have saved them well in excess of that amount. It costs us about $5/day (utilities, maintenance, insurance, and communications) to operate each of these units. With our 21 units in service, we will be saving these families a total of $525 for each day of operation. The volunteers keep the apartments filled over 99% of the time.

Beyond the physical plant, the spiritual and emotional support our volunteers graciously provide is impossible to measure. When asked how they can ever repay us, we simply admonish our guests to "pass it on."

We have no plans to expand our operations to other areas. Being a strictly volunteer organization, it would be impossible for us to go beyond the Texas Medical Center in Houston. However, we would be delighted to send more specific information to others who wish to develop similar operations in their localities. Already we know of one group in Oklahoma City that has plans to establish a Hospitality Apartment connected with a hospital there. This family stayed in one of our apartments while a sister lost the battle to cancer. The units they will build will be dedicated as a memorial to her. Having witnessed the enormous good this project has had on the lives of our guests, we hope that it can be replicated in many other places in the U.S.

For further information, contact

Human Resources Development Foundation
P.O. Box 1892
Houston, TX 77265-5213

Ministry to Public Servants

by John S. Lecky

John S. Lecky is Associate Pastor at Mountain Christian Church, Joppa, Maryland, where he works in Adult Ministries and Christian Education. He currently leads weekly Bible studies for state senators and delegates and coordinates the Prayer Breakfasts that take place during the legislative session. He has served on the staffs of two U.S. Senators, Mark Hatfield and William Brock.

The newspaper headlines read, "Governor pressured to resign due to alleged racketeering."

At six o'clock the lead story on the local news begins, "Senator . . . was indicted today on charges of bribery."

Rumors turn to action news reports when evidence is found linking a city official to organized crime. The news reaches millions, and they shake their heads at the corruption in politics.

"I'm sick and tired of being banged on by the press," complains an elected leader. "Why can't they ever pick up on something good we do?"

From another office down the hall comes deep feeling: "People just don't have any idea what our job is like down here. They think it's all glory. I've been spending eighteen hours a day on this over the past six months. It's tough!" From the perspective of the politician, misrepresentation and misunderstanding are formidable foes.

Politicians are real people. Yet because of their spotlighted position in society, the explosive issues that evoke great public emotion, and the media's zeal to provide the news to a consumer-oriented society, people in elected public life seldom are seen or treated as real people. Most in this professional field have come to accept this fact and consider it a cost of the course. Some good people steer clear of the course because of this peril. Others take advantage of their position, issues, and the media to the further propagation of the negative public perspective of politicians.

A great deal of darkness is associated with politics and government. True, corruption finds many opportunities in the field, and understanding of the people and the process of politics is often dim. Yet it's a mistake to believe that all in government leadership live in darkness. Because of the faith of some in the field, and the love of God for all who serve, there is reason to have hope for good in spite of the darkness we see.

While we send proclaimers of the Light of Christ into the spiritual darkness of Kenya and Zimbabwe, the church has been reluctant to go among politcians with the enlightening love of the Lord. Our light must shine in governments, in political parties, in the ruling processes of counties, states, and nations. With some measure of wisdom, caution says, "Let's not get involved in anything political, we'll be misunderstood," or, "It's a dirty business, and we've got so many other good concerns to address." Nonetheless, the greater part of wisdom will see the need for light in this area and realize the tremendous impact the light of the Lord can have in governments.

Successful ministries to people in public life now exist and have been taking place for some time. Yet the need exists for many more men and women who will become prepared for and active in this area of specialized ministry. Believers need to see the opportunity of ministry to real people in a profession where a very real possibility exists for positive changes in counties, states, and nations to the glory of God.

Biblical Teaching

Scripture gives us a direct call to honor and pray for our public servants. It also gives us a clear understanding of the nature of public leadership. Paul teaches in Romans 13 that leaders not only are to be honored, but understood as servants of God for the good of society. God has ordained government for the praise of good behavior and for the discipline of ones who do evil. In so doing, the leader of government then "is a minister of God to you for good" (Romans 13:4, NASB). How important it is that these people know the ordination and essential nature of their work!

Peter is no less sure of God's purpose and design for government. This apostle presents a parallel to Paul's Roman letter in 1 Peter 2:14. He writes that the king or governor is sent "for the punishment of evildoers and the praise of those who do right."

God has set forth a high purpose for any who would take the reins of leadership. Perhaps any generation of believers could respond by saying, "certainly our leaders are not functioning in these ways." But whether they do or not, believers ought to hold before their political leaders God's intention, design, and purpose for their tasks.

Able believers may also seek to become leaders of state to embody God's purposes among their colleagues in government.

Consider the leaders of state who in their greatest hours brought forth the ideals we have seen. Joseph in Egypt changed the course of history for the betterment of God's people. He was second in government only to the Pharaoh. David and Esther in their days of godly direction brought glory, peace, and tremendous development for the people of God's kingdom. Even in a state at first hostile to God, Daniel became one of the most influential leaders of the Babylonian world empire. These people served God with great success through governments of their day because they knew their God, they understood His purposes for their privilege and responsibility of leadership, and they depended upon His powerful presence to influence the directions they would take as political leaders.

To all who read the Bible the example of godly public leadership is presented in historic lives. We need to faithfully respond by becoming personally involved in special ministry to public servants.

Beginning the Ministry

Several members of the Mountain Christian Church came together to share concern for a number of elected leaders in our northern Maryland communities. From former associations, one of our members contacted Dr. Richard Halverson, Chaplain of the United States Senate. Because of our close proximity to Washington, D.C. and by his generous consent, our group was able to meet with him.

Chaplain Halverson's insights gave direction to the subsequent development of our ministry.

1. Persons disposed to this type of service should be prepared to commit themselves to faithful daily prayer for the individuals in leadership.

2. The commitment to personal intercession should be known by those for whom we pray. The leaders should be informed of the group's positive concern and intended support. In that first contact, we made sure to clarify our intention to serve, not to pressure as another special interest group.

3. Building a relationship of trust and fellowship between group members and government leaders was perhaps the best avenue toward providing an effective ministry.

We began with individuals serving in the Maryland State Legislature for the districts in which our congregation resides. While the President, Vice-President, the U.S. Senators and Representatives of Maryland, and other elected or appointed national leaders were also on our minds and in our prayers, the accessibility and approachability of our state senators and delegates to Annapolis made more likely the possibility of personal contact needed for this special ministry. We committed ourselves to know who these state legislators were, to select individuals for whom we would each faithfully pray, and to develop contact with them for the purposes suggested to us.

To accomplish that task we felt the need to form a group of persons like-minded in service. A task group came together for the special purpose of ministry to ones in public service. We informed the deacons and elders of the congregation about our group, for their information and support. Those in the group at the inception were joined by several others who shared a common concern.

Our task group for this ministry is diverse. We include a state police patrolman and his wife, a secretary at a local state police barracks; a pastor; a sixth-grade science teacher; the finance director for the county Board of Education and his wife, a music teacher; a major at an Army installation and his wife, an instructor at a community college currently serving as the president of the county Board of Education. Perhaps a common thread of concern for the well-being of our neighbors is to be found in each profession represented, but the strongest bond is the desire to be of service in the name of the Lord Jesus to those from our community who have been elected to lead our state.

Our small group agreed to make the following commitments:

1. Each person selected a leader for whom to pray faithfully, daily. Each one informed the leader of that commitment. Responses from our legislative leaders have been interesting, ranging from a startled (perhaps unbelieving) acknowledgment to a warm and grateful expression of need for such support. No leader responded negatively upon hearing of our support.

2. We would spend time together regularly. While almost daily many of us see each other, we set aside a monthly time for the specific purpose of updating each other on our experiences. Sometimes we invite a legislator to share that time with the group. Normally we plan group undertakings and usually dream together about possible developments of the ministry. A Saturday morning breakfast meeting has been the usual gathering occasion. Through our time of prayer, mutual support, and discussion of our common purpose and individual experiences in our tasks, our own group is drawing closer in Christian fellowship.

Opportunities

Some stimulating experiences have been shared relating to our ministry. The details are reserved and in some cases rearranged to assure a very important factor in this and every ministry—trust. While an outline of what the Lord is accomplishing is important to share, the confidences known in fellowship are always to be honored.

An experience with one legislator brought encouragement to the group. It shows that in crisis there is often reason for hope.

In the midst of a recent Savings and Loan crisis in Maryland, a member of the state legislature phoned one of the people in our group. This leader, who had at first seemed taken aback by the group's prayer commitment, called to say if ever the prayers were needed, it was then. Initiating the conversation, the legislator sought the prayers of the group member at a time of serious difficulty.

This leader is not a participating member of any local congregation of believers. Yet respect for prayer and gratitude for the group member's support were expressed. New kindnesses have been shared since this experience between the group and the legislator, for whom prayers continue daily.

Due to the pressures of office and conflict of priorities, good leaders sometimes leave public life. It seems the more conscientious one is, the more difficult is the pressure to respond to each constituent request, tackle a task left untouched by others, or spend additional hours studying to create solutions to complex issues. Those who are believers also feel strong commitment to family and faith, yet find these values in direct competition with the numerous demands before them. Those who deeply care about people for the sake of the Lord often have the hardest time remaining in a position that places so many competitive demands on their time.

Recently a respected and effective leader considered leaving public life for these reasons. Because of a strong faith this legislator placed high value on devotion to God's purposes and commitment to a quality family experience. Nevertheless, the elected position, combined with business obligations, encroached upon desired qualities in faith and family. With demands growing in each area, politics, business, faith, and family, resignation from public service seemed inevitable.

The fellowship our group had with this legislator was very special. We had already spent time together, inviting the legislator to speak to a church group, developing a closer relationship, before the most difficult period began. When the weight of the competing priorities came with its heaviest pressure, a basis of friendship had already been established between group members and the legislator. From that point on associations with the group deepened. When our ministry group learned that the weight of responsibilities had become a difficult burden for our friend, we intensified our efforts to help. Prayers were broadened from the one person's promise to the commitment of the entire group. One of the group members began spending regular time with the legislator in moments of listening, sharing Scripture, and personal prayer. Time was spent with the family in the home in a circle of searching for God's will. We consulted with several strong Christian brothers in public life, who imparted wisdom and encouragement to our friend. Group members sent notes, made calls, and consulted together to offer encouragement during these difficult days.

Through the course of weeks, God's will became more apparent. The strong desire in our friend's heart to serve the Lord through governmental leadership became a clearer driving force. Numerous Christian individuals offered encouragement for continuation in elected leadership. Business concerns began to be resolved and fade from primary consideration. Our friend could see horizons that offered more home and family time. Possibilities grew for greater support from other people of faith in elected positions.

The decision was made to remain in public life, but the most exciting aspect was the conviction behind the decision. The legislator determined to remain in elected office for the sake of the Lord, considering that position a personal ministry. In later conversations with others in similar office, the legislator said, "the only reason I'm here is because this is what I believe the Lord wants me to do."

Since that point there have been many affirmations for that decision. Opportunities to serve the Lord from the elected position continue to increase, and Christians from many corners have expressed gratitude for our friend's conviction.

Still the pressures of office remain, though they are viewed with the conviction that God's grace is sufficient to meet the needs of one whose life is devoted to His ministry. Such an individual is a bright light in a dark place. Perhaps here is one of the Josephs or Daniels we so desperately need.

Future Plans

The next step for our group will be to get to know more personally all of the members of the state legislature governing us directly. They, their families, their convictions, and their concerns are of primary interest to us. Especially leading up to and during the ninety-day General Assembly (January—March), ministry to and with these individuals will take priority.

During the times of the year when the legislature is in recess, other possible activities are envisioned. More personal fellowship with our group will be possible in the district when legislators are in home territory. From such times together with ones we know less well, we will learn what appropriate ministries we can provide. To better acquaint the congregation with the state representatives, the group has considered hosting neighborhood receptions or coffees. We feel it important that members of the congregation know those elected to serve them. We have also provided names, addresses, phone numbers, and ways of contacting better knowledge of and access to them. Finally, for election years, forums for the candidates are being considered. Herein are opportunities for church members to know firsthand the positions, convictions, and personalities of those who vie for office.

We will continue to watch for the potential Josephs and Daniels of our time. While we minister to current leaders we will also work to develop Christian statesmen for the future. Both are needed ministries.

The world is transformed by ministry. All who serve in the name of the Lord Jesus Christ continue His ministry on earth. His people have been called to go forth as lights into a world of darkness. So will go believers who minister to people in public service. The challenge is to illumine those who can transform the world to the glory of God the Father.

Some Suggestions

1. If the elected official is a Christian, offer support. Encourage, teach, pray, serve, or simply be available.
2. If the leader is not a Christian, show the love of Christ. Develop a basis of friendship, help where possible, let them know you, and help them to know Christ.

3. Remember the servant role. In a group as outlined, never lobby or exist as a special interest group.
4. Be open to all persons; avoid partisanship. Never use relationships established for political maneuvering.
5. Be sensitive to time. The ministry is serious, but so are demands of leaders' schedules.
6. Be concerned for the whole life of the leader. God is. Let your ministry be as holistic as possible. Remember the staff, family, friends, and colleagues of the leader.
7. Watch out for glory. Be sure to give it to God.

Further Reading

Decision Editors, "God's Servant in the Senate—An Interview with Richard C. Halverson." *Decision* Magazine, January, 1985.

Charles Colson, *Born Again.* Chosen/Zondervan, 1976.

Peter L. Benson and Dorothy L. Williams, *Religion on Capitol Hill.* San Francisco: Harper and Row, 1982.

Hospice

by Dale R. Fjeran and Janice Weaver

Dale R. Fjeran is formerly the director of the hospice at Southwest Christian Church, East Point, Georgia, and was instrumental in its administrative operation until his recent retirement. Janice Weaver, B.S.N., is a registered nurse who works as Patient Care Coordinator and Acting Director.

Hospice care strives to provide a personalized experience of death for the terminal patient and his or her family. The Southwest Christian Hospice is dedicated to loving people and to affirming life, so that we "do not grieve like the rest of men, who have no hope" (1 Thessalonians 4:13b).

In an institutional setting, care provided for the terminal patient can become so routine that he and his family are deprived of the dignity and freedom to experience and handle death as they might in the home setting. However, the desire to spend one's last days at home may be offset by the need for expert nursing and medical care, or by the burden that home care places on the family and friends. This is where a hospice comes in—relieving the burden of home care.

Mrs. Johnson (name changed) was a 76-year-old lady who was referred to our hospice by the American Cancer Society. She had been diagnosed one year before with cancer of the colon and liver, and surgery and chemotherapy had failed to halt the spread of her disease. She had moved from her hometown to live with her son and granddaughter, and had been caring for herself until her disease progressed to the point that more help was needed. It was at this point that hospice became involved.

One the first visit to the home by the hospice nurse, she was found to be weak, emaciated and in pain, but she assured the nurse that she was doing "pretty well." It was soon apparent that she never complained to her family about her illness, and only when the pain became unbearable would she be willing to take medication that would relieve it.

Mrs. Johnson was from a small town in south Georgia and had three older sisters. These sisters came faithfully every weekend and cleaned house and prepared food for the following week. So it was determined that her greatest need for help was during the week when her son was working and her granddaughter was in school.

We assigned three volunteers to Mrs. Johnson, one who was a nurse volunteer as well as two others. These volunteers made regular visits to the family, and performed such tasks as running errands, doing housework, shampooing Mrs. Johnson's hair or simply sitting with her while her family members got some much needed rest. As Mrs. Johnson's disease worsened, she became unable to swallow her pain medication and the problem of unrelieved pain became critical. The nurse volunteer, however, had the solution for this problem: simply teach a family member to give her an injection. With the doctor's permission, we obtained injectable drugs, and this hardy volunteer not only taught injection technique, but also allowed the family to practice on her own arm!

Another need that hospice was able to meet for Mrs. Johnson was her desire for pastoral visits for Bible reading and prayer. Since she had not been in our area long, she had not established a church home although she professed an active Christian faith. Thus, having no local minister, our ministerial staff visited her as they are happy to do for any hospice patient who requests spiritual care.

We were also able to provide Mrs. Johnson with needed supplies such as nutritional supplements, disposable bed pads, bedside commode, wheelchair, in-bed shampoo tray, adult diapers and other items as the need arose.

As Mrs. Johnson became weaker and sicker, she begun to tell her family members that she was ready to go home to be with her Lord, and that she hoped that it would be soon. In a few days, she lapsed into a coma, and at this point the family requested that someone from hospice come and stay in the home until death occurred. The hospice nurse came and stayed with the family, calming their fears and assuring them that all that was needed now was that they be by her side and telling her of their love for her, even though it appeared she was no longer hearing them.

Mrs. Johnson died peacefully about 12 hours later, in her own bed, surrounded by all her sisters, all but one of her children, and one of her grandchildren. She was surrounded by love until her very last breath.

Setting Up

When we began to set up our hospice ministry in 1983, there were no established state guidelines, but the governor of Georgia had appointed a task force to draw up preliminary guidelines that eventually resulted in a Hospice Licensure Law for the state of Georgia, enacted in 1984. We were surveyed by the state in August, 1984 and were at that time granted our state license. We are re-surveyed yearly.

The state requirements contain several areas that would be basic to any hospice program:

1. A governing body
2. An advisory board
3. An administrator
4. A medical director
5. A nurse
6. A social worker
7. A counselor (family, pastoral, etc.)
8. Volunteers
9. Availability 24 hours per day, seven days per week
10. Bereavement services
11. Provision for in-patient care (usually through contracts with hospitals or nursing homes)

12. Provision for obtaining supplies and equipment
13. A written manual of policies and procedures

The governing body was formed by the Trustees of Southwest Christian Church. The advisory board was comprised of people from the business, medical, and helping professions familiar with the work of our church. Our medical director is a licensed physician and a member of the church. Our nurse is our Patient Care Coordinator, who makes the home care segment of our ministry run smoothly. The social worker is a licensed Master Social Worker and is responsible for providing a full range of supportive services to the patient and family. Counseling is mostly provided by the church ministers, while any special counseling needs are referred to a professional counselor (also a volunteer).

The volunteers carry the real load; without them there would be no program. At present there are only two paid staff members in our hospice, Director and Patient Care Coordinator. All others donate their services.

One requirement to being licensed by the state was the writing of a policy and procedures manual. This manual describes the hospice's goals, methods by which those goals are sought, and mechanisms by which the basic hospice care services are delievered.

In addition to state regulations, many hospice organizations in our area attempted to meet federal regulations in order to qualify for cost reimbursement from Medicare. We meet the Medicare requirements but choose not to become involved because of the large volume of paperwork involved.

It is, of course, possible to do the work of a hospice organization without calling it such. Most hospitals, due to recent changes in Medicare reimbursement, do not keep patients diagnosed as terminal (and therefore no longer under active treatment) and they are released to go home. Often it is difficult or expensive for a family to care for a terminally ill member at any place other than home, and there it can be a strain on the family. Your church may already have a ministry of caring for members who are sick at home; with some broadening your ministry can become a hospice ministry. If it is not formally called a "hospice," it may not be subject to state regulations. At present, seventeen states have hospice laws and thirteen more have drafts or are considering such legislation. to find out whether your state has a hospice law, contact

The National Hospice Organization
Suite 202
1901 North Fort Myer Dr.
Arlington, VA 22209

Personnel

Many kinds of workers are essential to our hospice ministry. One is our Patient Care Coordinator. She is a registered nurse whose main responsibility is making the home care segment of the program function smoothly. She visits each patient a minimum of once a week (daily if necessary) and is responsible for assigning volunteers to the home care patients and scheduling their visits. She is on call twenty-four hours a day, which can become very taxing.

The most important group is the volunteers. This congregation is blessed with many people who have the gift of service or mercy, so necessary in maintaining a volunteer staff. Our volunteers are assigned two to a patient and they each give at least four hours per week to that patient. They have been faithful in serving the needs of others in every way—caring for patients, running errands, cleaning house, cooking meals, providing transportation, or doing maintenance work. They also serve as companions and provide respite time for the family members. They all respond when called upon. The Lord has truly blessed us in these people.

When we first surveyed our congregation for volunteers, we received over 60 responses. Our next step was to prepare them for service by putting together a meaningful training seminar. We did this with the assistance of a neighboring hospice and from literature available on hospice activities in the U.S.

We organized a program of eight two-hour training sessions that met on Wednesday nights. The sessions covered an introduction to the hospice ministry, physician-patient communications, death and dying, supportive and social services review, volunteer policies and the role of the volunteer, home care, spiritual aspects of the hospice, and the bereavement program. Fifty-seven volunteers completed the course and were awarded a special certificate.

The volunteers continue to meet twice a month. The meetings have a twofold purpose—the provide a time for the volunteers to air their feelings, and they allow time for in-service training (as required by state regulation).

How It Works

Our patients come from all walks of life. They are referred to us by hospital social workers, attending physicians, family members, nursing groups, ministers, the American Cancer Society, other hospice groups, and by word of mouth. We review each referral carefully to determine if they meet certain initial criteria before we begin assessing their individual needs. These criteria are:

1. A prognosis from the attending physician of a life expectancy of six months or less.

2. The knowledge of their terminal diagnosis and the desire to have our services.

3. The consent of the attending physician.

4. Residence within an established geographical area (this is done so that we will not spread our resources too thin).

The needs of the patient and family are assessed by members of the team following the approval of the patients attending physician. At all times the hospice works in conjunction with the physician, not apart from him or her. Initially, our hospice focused its work with the patient and family in their homes, providing nursing care, family counseling, sharing with the family, social services, various volunteer services, and bereavement care. Those that could no longer be cared for at home were admitted to a hospital or a terminal care center.

Now, however, construction of an eight-bed, in-patient facility is under way, with a projected completion time of August 1986. The in-patient facility will serve three basic functions: A place for the patient to come temporarily for symptom control (pain, nausea, vomiting, etc.); a place for the patient to come for a few days to one week to give home caregivers a time of respite; and a place for patients who can no longer be managed at home or whose families request that the death not occur at home. The hospice building will project a home-like atmosphere, with each room housing only one patient with provision for family members to stay overnight. Visitors may come and go at will, and will have access to a fully-equipped kitchen for preparation of special meals or treats as desired. Most rooms will have patios where beds or wheelchairs may be moved as weather and patient condition permits.

Our entire program is financed by this congregation. The majority of the hospice programs in our area receive their funds through community fund drives, private solicitation, the United Way, or Medicare. We make no charge for our services. At present, we are able to meet the needs of all our patients, whatever the needs may be. We have available for our patients such items as hospital beds, wheel chairs, bedside commodes, tub chairs, walkers, canes, crutches, absorbent pads, dressings, catheters, etc. If the patient has a need for an item we don't have, it will be rented at our expense.

Our hospice maintains office hours from 8:30 a.m. to 12:30 p.m. Monday through Friday. On afternoons and weekends all hospice calls are recorded on the answering machine, which alerts the hospice nurse carrying the electronic pager. All calls are returned as soon as possible.

The routine of the hospice varies from day to day, and we serve seven or eight people in a typical week. Patients to be visited are seen by the nurse or a volunteer. Patients needing transportation to their doctor's office or to a hospital as outpatients are scheduled for pickup. Calls taken for new referrals are processed.

We are not a large congregation compared to some, with an average attendance of 900, though we are larger than the average. The size of a congregation is a secondary consideration to the starting of a hospice program. The desire to serve is vital. Granted, congregations that are few in number would find it difficult to undertake such a ministry on their own. But that would not preclude them from forming a consortium of churches in the area that would have a similar interest to launch such a program.

The hospice ministry is, in a word, rewarding. Staff and volunteers alike become very close to those we serve and their hurts and fears become a part of us. It is through the Lord's loving guidance that He brings us through the difficult times. However, the blessings attained far outweigh the tears shed.

Ministry to Refugees

by Marjorie Miller

Marjorie Miller is Publicist and Acquisitions Editor at Standard Publishing. She is a member of the New Burlington Church of Christ in Cincinnati, Ohio, where she teaches a class of women and is actively involved in their women's ministries.

"I've been wanting to talk with you," said a man in my congregation. "Do you know La?"

"Yes."

"La needs someplace to stay. They've been beating on her."

La is a Cambodian refugee. She had been attending our church along with about twenty-five other refugees. I wasn't sure who had been beating on her, nor did I ever find out for certain. But as I pictured the small dark-haired girl with the pretty smile and the haunting brown eyes, I knew what my answer must be.

Two days later, La brought everything she owned in two garbage bags, and I became her mom. She has been with me for seven months now. During that time, she has learned many things—and so have I!

One of the major hurdles in building a relationship with a person from another country is the language barrier. But it is amazing how much fun it is to learn new arts of communication and how few times we have really been unable to understand one another.

La is 24 years old. She is a serious student. She wants to learn to speak (and read and write) English. Three mornings a week she attends the English classes that are offered for the refugees in our city. And we sometimes study together for several hours in the evening.

When La first came, I would read and explain the Bible to her, and she would listen. Then she began to repeat after me, phrase by phrase, as I read. Now, she reads, and I help her with unfamiliar words. Often when I come home from work, I will find her stretched out on the floor with two editions of the *Life of Christ Visualized* (English and Cambodian) in front of her. There are many things she does not understand. But she is intrigued with the magic of learning new words, excited when she discovers she can put them together to express her own thoughts, and especially happy that she can read for herself "what God says."

A second barrier, often even more difficult to penetrate, is the difference in cultural background. By definition, a refugee is a person for whom it would be dangerous to return to his or her native land. La escaped to Thailand after the death of her parents. But she, like most refugees, is proud of her country and clings to certain memories and customs.

Her tastes in food, clothing, TV programs, and room decoration are different from mine. In general, I have not tried to impose my personal preferences upon her. I have out of necessity, however, had to teach her such things as regard for time and schedules, the basics of acceptable behavior, and the wise use of money.

Mutual respect, love, and candid discussion sprinkled with a generous portion of patience will usually result in an acceptable solution to the little problems that could lead to big problems.

One of the greatest frustrations, challenges—sacrifices, if you please—is the lack of privacy. La is very dependent. She is from a large family, she has lived in an apartment with a number of people, and she wants (needs?) to be with me and to know what I'm doing all of the time. When La first came to live with me, she was full of fear. Many of the fears have gone now. Others are fading. Perhaps, as she becomes more independent and self-confident, this inconvenience too will be resolved. In the meantime, the knowledge that someone is watching and mimicking my every act has made me a better person.

Getting Started

My church's refugee ministry started in the mind of one man when he saw a TV ad for sponsors for boat people. He shared the idea with our minister. The minister preached a series of sermons on the responsibility of Christians to care for the homeless and the hungry, and the congregation was challenged to accept the sponsorship of a family.

Several of our members accepted the challenge. One man owned an apartment building, and the others began to equip one of the apartments for the arrival of the refugee family. A checklist was made of the necessities, and various people volunteered for specific duties. What a lovely welcome that refugee family received! They knew little about America and American ways, but they must have sensed the love of Christ in the many people who ministered to their needs.

Since the first family, there have been many others. Another man in our congregation purchased an apartment building for the purpose of providing housing for refugees. He and his wife live in one apartment, and the other rooms are occupied by the refugees.

Becoming a Sponsor

A number of organizations and agencies are involved in refugee services. We have found the Refugee Services Division of World Relief to be most helpful.

The first thing a church or an individual who wishes to become a sponsor should do is to request (from the address on page 128 or another organization) a Refugee Sponsor Form. You will be asked to sign a commitment form stating that you will "assist in the resettlement of a refugee family with the goal of helping that family to become self-supporting, contributing members of the community as quickly as possible."

If you are accepted as a sponsor, World Relief will provide assistance in helping you prepare for your sponsorship. Two booklets that are extremely helpful to the new sponsor are

"The Challenge of Sponsorship" and an Ethnic Profile on the background from which your particular people come (Ethiopian, Cambodian, etc.). Some of the information provided relates to the goals of sponsorship, preparation for arrival, sponsor-refugee relationships, tips on orientation of the refugees, and suggestions for helping the refugees to adjust to life in America.

A Refugee Orientation Manual called "Starting Again!" is provided as a guide to the refugees. This booklet is helpful to sponsors as well, as it explains legal requirements, immigration procedures, health care, education, welfare assistance, and other basic information. Local agencies such as the Department of Human Services, Immigration and Naturalization, and your Post Office can help you find answers to some of your questions. Cincinnati has a Cambodian Association, which assists the refugees in applying for financial aid, education, and employment.

When your refugees arrive, they come with the clothes on their backs and a 12" x 18" box in which they have brought their most prized possessions. Often the box contains food, because they have a fear of starvation. They should have an I-94 identification form, given to them before they left their asylum country, as proof that they have been admitted to the United States as a "Parolee," and are allowed to work and stay here for an indefinite period of time. It is advisable for the sponsor to make copies of this form for the refugee to carry and keep the original in a safe place.

As soon as possible, someone needs to get Social Security cards for them, get the children enrolled in school, sign them up for welfare and food stamps (unless you have been able to get a job for them), get a medical card, and take them to a clinic for physical checkups. (Everyone is required to have a chest X ray and be checked for tuberculosis, venereal disease, and other communicable diseases before entering the United States, and everyone is required to have a checkup here within ninety days after his/her arrival.)

The task of being a sponsor is time-consuming, and the demands go far beyond performing the necessary details. For this reason, it is wise to have a support group who will share in the various functions as well as spend time in orientation, tutoring, and being friends. We have had some financial assistance, some donations, and some grants from refugee service organizations. A Bible college has provided translators, videos, tapes, Bibles, songbooks, filmstrips, and scholarships for refugees. But the real key to success with refugees, as with any other contact, is to be friends with them. People need to visit them, invite them into their homes, and talk with them about American customs. Christians need to help them know about God, His Word, and His Son.

Expectations

Not everyone in our congregation is excited about the Cambodian ministry. We have lost some members. Some are opposed to spending time and money on "foreigners." Some are uncomfortable with cultural differences. Some have been disappointed because of unrealistic expectations.

In spite of all the helpful information that is available, there will probably be unrealistic expectations on the part of both the sponsor and the refugee.

Many of the refugees expect to have a good job and/or free education awaiting them when they step off the plane. Some think everybody in America is rich. Others are disappointed to learn that not everyone is waiting to receive them with open arms and financial assistance.

People who have sponsored the refugees expect them to settle down and become happy, contented, stable Americans. They are disappointed when the refugee, to whom they have given so much of themselves, suddenly moves away to join relatives in another part of the country or seek another location more like his or her native land.

In general, the refugees at first are overly dependent. Then, after several months, perhaps even a year, they may go through a period of rebellion in which they seem to flaunt their independence. Only as sponsors are able to look at two of their main goals—to give the refugees freedom and to lead them to self-suffiency—can they realize they have really achieved these goals.

In this ministry, as in many others, there is not always one clear-cut method that leads to success. For instance, there is a difference of opinion about the best way to provide Bible knowledge and worship experiences for the refugee. Some believe the refugees should have their own congregations. Others feel it is advantageous to incorporate them into American churches. We have tried to include some studies (home Bible studies and a Sunday-school class) especially for Cambodians, but to have all meet together in the worship services. This, we feel, enables them to learn in their own language and enjoy a special fellowship with their own people. At the same time, it promotes unity and mutual acceptance between the refugee constituency and the sponsoring American congregation.

Most of our refugees say they are Christians. Some may say this because they believe it will give them preferential treatment. Others know a little bit about Christianity or have observed that the people who reach out to them in love are Christians. But their knowledge of the Bible is minimal. They need to be taught. Most of all, they need to see the indwelling of Christ in the lives of their teachers.

Cambodians, like Americans, are free to choose their religion. Just because a Christian church sponsors a refugee does not mean that he or she will automatically become a Christian. They are soon exposed to the American gods of pleasure and greed, and the Buddhists are making a concentrated effort to win them too.

Most of the refugee children are good students. They are rapidly learning the language and the customs of their new country. It is not unreasonable to anticipate that they can make an important contribution to the future of America and the church as they bring with them the same kind of ambition, excitement, and resourcefulness that the European immigrants of a few years ago brought with them.

The refugee ministry is not easy. It demands time, money, energy, and patience. But as I talked with those of our congregation who have carried the heaviest loads, they agreed that the last few years have been the happiest years of their lives. As one man and his wife expressed it, "We've gotten more than we've given. If we had fifty apartments, we would fill them all with refugees. Being missionaries in our own city is more rewarding than we ever dreamed."

For more information, write
Refugee Services Division
World Relief
P.O. Box WRC,
Nyack, NY 10960

Phone (800) 431-2808 or (914) 268-4135